KNOWLEDGE TRANSFER BY INDUSTRIAL SECURITY PERSONNEL AT A UNITED STATES-BASED AEROSPACE COMPANY:
A PHENOMENOLOGICAL STUDY

Michael R. Perez, D.M.

Author: **Michael R. Perez, D.M.**
               Whittier, CA 90601

Publisher: **Dawn D. Boyer, M.Ad.Ed., Ph.D., D. Boyer**
               Consulting
               Virginia Beach, VA 23464; Dawn.Boyer@me.com

Copyright ©   2014 – Original Dissertation
               2015 – Commercial Conversion
ISBN Numbers   ISBN-13: 978-1517205898
               ISBN-10: 1517205891

Disclaimer:

The author has attempted to gather as much of the facts and information to the utmost complete and truthfulness for the compilation of this book from bona fide sources, Internet sources, printed material in currently circulating and non-circulating sources, literature review, newspaper articles, and personal interviews. Dates noted were from publically available sources.

Keep in mind – any data included (or left out, incorrectly quoted, or attributed) may be attributed to transcription errors or types. Several bodies of research were interpretations of the same or original documents and errors might have occurred as transcribed. Anyone with more data to contribute to a future, updated, and corrected version of this research project is encouraged to send materials to the author's email address noted above.

Connect to the Author

LinkedIn profile: www.linkedin.com/in/michaelperez5

This text has been altered in format from the original dissertation document to conform to easier to read for the general public and commercial publishing standards. Scholars reviewing the contents and formatting for standardization for thesis or dissertation should *not* use this book's current formatting as a model. Please see your school's guidelines for the acceptable formatting for the graduate level thesis researched. Alternatively, consult with a professional academic editor for completing your publication.

TABLE OF CONTENTS

LIST OF TABLES

LIST OF FIGURES

DEDICATION & ACKNOWLEDGEMENTS

This dissertation is dedicated to the special woman in my life, Tracy Ann Rico, for inspiring and encouraging me to complete this journey. She has supported and encouraged me throughout this process while putting our life on hold since 2008. I cannot ask for more in a companion, friend, and confidant. To my children, who have supported me during this journey, and whom I love tremendously Michelle R. Perez, Jessica L. Perez, and Michael R. Perez II. Their continued support and inspiration helped me to be a role model to them as they pursue their educational aspirations. To my parents James and Marie Perez for modeling a work ethic that inspired me throughout my 29 years of service with the United States-based aerospace company as depicted in this study.

Additionally, I would like to thank my friends and family members who have stood by me when my journey became overwhelming. I would like to take this opportunity to thank my committee chair, Dr. Gerald W. Olivas, who inspired and encouraged me, step-by-step throughout this journey. I would like to thank Dr. Olivas for his guidance, feedback, and patience helping me throughout this process. I am indebted to him for his constant support and encouraging words that meant so much when times became tough. His constant guidance helped me to remain focused on each step throughout this process.

To my committee members, Dr. Regina Sadono, and Dr. Sean Gyll, thanks for your guidance, support, and feedback. I would like to thank my Academic Representative, Kurt Boyd, and my Financial Advisor Jen Kuskie for your support and guidance throughout this journey. Your guidance helped me stay on track by providing updated financial and academic progress throughout this journey.

Michael R. Perez, D.M.

KNOWLEDGE TRANSFER BY INDUSTRIAL SECURITY PERSONNEL AT A UNITED STATES-BASED AEROSPACE COMPANY: A PHENOMENOLOGICAL STUDY

by

Michael R. Perez, D.M.

2014, Doctor of Management, Organizational
Leadership, University of Phoenix, AZ
1994, Master of Public Administration,
California State University Fullerton, Fullerton, CA
1988, Bachelor of Science, Criminal Justice,
California State University Long Beach, Long Beach,
CA
1980, Associate Arts, Cypress College, Cypress, CA

A Dissertation Submitted to the Faculty of University
of Phoenix in Partial Fulfillment of the Requirements
for the Degree of

**Doctor Of Management in
Organizational Leadership**

University of Phoenix, AZ

Gerald W. Olivas, Ed.D., Chair
Regina Sadono, Ph.D., Committee Member
Sean Gyll, Ph.D., Committee Member
Jeremy Moreland, Ph.D., Dean, School of Advanced Studies

Approved: November 17, 2014

ABSTRACT

KNOWLEDGE TRANSFER BY INDUSTRIAL SECURITY PERSONNEL AT A UNITED STATES-BASED AEROSPACE COMPANY: A PHENOMENOLOGICAL STUDY

Michael R. Perez, D.M.
University of Phoenix, AZ
2014

Jeremy Moreland, Ph.D., Dean, School of Advanced Studies
Gerald W. Olivas, Ed.D., Chair

Corporations are experiencing significant changes because of the impending Baby Boomers retirements. There are four generations in the workforce today, Traditionalist, Baby Boomers, and Generations X and Y. To effectively address the knowledge management challenges organizations are creating mechanisms to identify, capture, and transfer knowledge to individuals who will be tasked with replacing Baby Boomers, the largest segment of the population. This phenomenological study addressed organizational readiness and loss of knowledge when Baby Boomers retire from the United States-based aerospace company.

Twenty semi-structured, face-to-face and telephone interviews were conducted at the United States-based aerospace company. The major findings from this research study identified the need to implement a knowledge transfer program, filling the intermediate gap of security personnel, motivating remaining employees, providing incentives for sharing knowledge, and addressing the obstacles toward knowledge sharing. More important, leaders face the challenge of having skilled and qualified personnel in place before Baby Boomers retire from the organization. In addition, the lack of a robust knowledge transfer program was a finding that requires attention from all leaders, to ensure the company's competitive advantage is not threatened.

It will be imperative for security leaders to ensure knowledge transfer occurs in the organization once Baby Boomers begin to retire. Knowledge sharing with less experienced personnel is critical to providing security leaders with insight into identifying, capturing, and transferring industrial security knowledge before Baby Boomers retire, thus sustaining the organization's competitive advantage. Future research in the area of information technology is important to building a robust infrastructure to support knowledge management in the security and fire protection organization.

CHAPTER I

Introduction

Leaders and managers are in a precarious position of managing an aging population as Baby Boomers, the largest group of knowledge workers around the world begin to retire. A transformation is happening in the labor force around the country as Baby Boomers (people born between the years 1946-1964) retire from their organizations. As the largest group of knowledge workers, Baby Boomer retirements are becoming a reality in many American organizations causing leaders to revisit or create knowledge management systems. The implications of losing qualified and experienced personnel are daunting. Organizations can expect to have knowledge disappear as experienced workers, who make up 25% of the United States workforce begin to retire (Dalkir, 2011). The loss of workplace knowledge creates a crisis in strategy for organizations that must stay competitive in a global economy. The Baby Boomer exodus from the workforce is a global concern, not merely isolated to the United States. Population declines of 14% to 25% were occurring in Germany, Italy, and Spain according to United Nations Population Division (DeLong, 2004). Therefore, the transfer of tacit knowledge from departing employees will become a strategic imperative because of cost and time constraints (Peet, Walsh, Sober, & Rawak, 2010).

An early retirement incentive plan could lead to a mass exodus of experienced talent, leaving organizations vulnerable, and unable to compete in an already difficult economy. Therefore, a cross-generational workforce should be educated and developed prior to any large-scale departures. Thus, organizations have the challenge of leveraging knowledge from an aging workforce. The combination of a surge in retirements and a growing reliance on unskilled multi-generational employees could cause long-term problems in the delivery of industrial security services to many Department of Defense (DoD) programs. In particular, the DoD programs currently under contract with the United States-based aerospace company could face a skills gap when experienced personnel take critical experience and experiential knowledge with them as they depart their organization. The retirement of 76 million Baby Boomers has the potential for huge losses of critical and technical knowledge because of a scarcity of talent (O'Dell & Hubert, 2011). Consequently, leaders and managers must have the ability to distinguish between what knowledge to retain or discard. Empson's (2001) typology of knowledge described technical and client knowledge within knowledge intensive firms. The sub-categories within technical knowledge are sectorial or shared at the sectorial level, organizational-company specific knowledge, and individual knowledge-personal knowledge acquired from education or work experience (as cited in Hislop, 2009). However, client knowledge sub-categories encompass the following: company specific knowledge – understanding of the company culture, and individuals – or having knowledge and acquaintance with key personnel in an organization (Hislop, 2009).

The definition of knowledge is experience, values, and information (Gagné, 2009). Lost knowledge can lead to reduced capacity to innovate, threaten growth strategies, competitor advantage, and increased vulnerability (DeLong, 2004). An organization's competitive advantage depends on employee motivation to share knowledge. An organization's objective is to share knowledge among its constituents; however, before knowledge sharing can occur, knowledge will be translated from tacit to explicit (Hislop, 2009). Codified (explicit) knowledge is protected by patents and intellectual property rights, and is held and shared by individual workers so that it becomes part of the knowledge base of the organization (Dalkir, 2011). Leaders emphasize cultivating a knowledge sharing culture by engaging, communicating with, and rewarding employees, building the program and culture (O'Dell & Hubert, 2011). However, organizational leaders and managers must distinguish tacit from explicit knowledge. According to Dalkir (2011), tacit knowledge is knowledge that is difficult to put into words, texts, or drawings making it difficult to codify. Bratianu and Orzea (2010) posited that tacit knowledge is learned through direct experience, feelings, intuitions, beliefs, and cultural values from interaction between individuals and the environment. Knowledge management is the practice that simplifies the management and sharing of information that is translated into knowledge (O'Sullivan & Dooley, 2009). The ability to share knowledge across the organization contributes to increased organizational performance, and the more knowledge shared across organizational boundaries, the more knowledge will be put to use (Dinur, 2011). The transformation of organizations into knowledge-oriented firms requires strategies to use knowledge that stimulate learning at later stages (Soliman, 2011).

The successful implementation of organizational knowledge management systems depends on the employees' motivation to share knowledge (Gagné, 2009). Knowledge sharing through a community of practice among organizational members is critical for an organization to develop the employee skills and abilities to sustain a competitive advantage (Buckley & Giannakopoulos, 2011). Employee retirements add to the importance of creating and sharing knowledge and shaping knowledge management systems in global organizations. In the global economy, organizational focus on knowledge creation and sharing can be critical to an organization's ability to sustain a competitive advantage. An effective knowledge management system can provide employees with required knowledge to help them perform tasks and make better decisions (Amirkhani, Tajmirriahi, Mohammadi, & Dalir, 2012). However, any reluctance to share knowledge among organizational members can lead to a skills gap among multi-generational employees.

The inability to share knowledge among industrial security employees at the aerospace company could have ramifications on national security. The inability to share knowledge suggests that workers are giving up their individual power and status (Hislop, 2013). If workers believe that sharing knowledge is good for themselves and the company they can have a positive effect toward sharing knowledge in their organizations. Hokanson, Sosa-Fey, and Vinaja (2011) stated, "Businesses globally are on the cusp of facing a new challenge – how to mitigate the effects of aging workforces and the coming loss of the Baby Boomer Generation through retirements" (p. 139). An additional challenge facing leaders is the integration and motivation of Traditional, Baby Boomers, Generation X, and Generation Y employees into the workplace. In the corporate environment, cross-generational personnel have to co-exist, with each bringing different assets and leadership style preferences to the workplace (Simons, 2010). Managers must learn to work with multi-generational employees who have different values (Murphy, Gibson, & Greenwood, 2010). Personnel movement in organizations can ease the transfer of tacit and explicit knowledge (Tuan, 2011). In this scenario, group members are more inclined to adopt a routine from rotating members when it was superior to their own (Tuan, 2011).

Chapter 1 of the study began with a dialogue of the necessity and importance of the research. Chapter 1 included the following information: the background of the problem, statement of the problem, purpose of the study, significance of the study, significance of the study to leadership, nature of the study, overview of the research method, overview of the design appropriateness, pilot study, research questions, the conceptual framework, and definition of terms. The chapter ended with a dialogue on the assumptions, scope and limitations, delimitations, summary to address the topic and problem, and a synopsis of the study.

Background of the Problem

The general problem is the inability to capture and share knowledge among workers leading to a knowledge and skills gap within United States-based corporations affecting their competitive advantage and ability to compete globally. A contributing factor affecting all industries is the gap (9.7 million) between Baby Boomers and Generation X workers (Reester, 2008). DeLong (2004) posited that organizational age demographics coupled with historical retirement rates contribute to the loss of human capital affecting the competitive advantage of United States company's. The complexity of organizations due to technology advancements requires knowledge workers limited time to digest and analyze information (Dalkir, 2011). The recent global economic collapse occurring between the years 2007 and 2009, and the (DoD) budget reductions, contributed to government program closures, along with a reduction in workforce

through attrition and retirements that affected the
delivery of services to the aerospace company
commercial and classified programs. The goal of
leadership is to have knowledge transfer throughout
the organization to include the culture, leadership,
and individual participants (Draghici & Petcu, 2011).

As a phenomenological researcher, the study
examined the lived experiences and perceptions of
industrial security managers and industrial security
specialists at an aerospace company to explore
organizational readiness when Baby Boomers retire,
and a loss of knowledge among subject matter
experts. The findings from the study have contributed
to existing knowledge management theory. The
phenomenological study conducted at the aerospace
company's industrial security organization added to
knowledge management literature by understanding
the obstacles to sharing knowledge among security
professionals supporting classified and intelligence
communities. Furthermore, impediments to
knowledge sharing could threaten national security if
industrial security leaders fail to create a knowledge
management culture. Additionally, the researcher
examined how prepared leaders are in creating and

sharing knowledge within an industrial security organization, as the lack of cross-generational knowledge sharing can contribute to the company's skills gap and loss of competitive advantage in a difficult economic market. Further, the motivation to share knowledge is seldom money, but more about an individual's reputation, reciprocity, and altruism (Shin- Yuan, Hui-Min, & Wen-Wen, 2011).

A manufacturer of commercial jetliners and military aircraft, the United States-based aerospace company, was carefully selected for this qualitative study, to understand the phenomenon under study. The aerospace company, based in Chicago, Illinois, employs workers in the United States and globally. The aerospace company industrial security services are delivered through the Shared Services Group (SSG), which includes the Security and Fire Protection (S&FP) group of 1,392 personnel encompassing the industrial security organization of approximately 550 industrial security personnel. The remaining 842 employees reside within the S&FP organization supporting the following functions: Executive Protection, BCA Infrastructure Security, Business Continuity, Domestic Security, Enterprise

Fire Protection, Uniformed Security, and International Security.

Knowledge transfer in organizations is the sharing of ideas across boundaries either internally or externally (Petkovic & Miric, 2009). Knowledge sharing is critical to employee learning, growth, and development. Srivastava (2011) stated, "Knowledge sharing acts as a catalyst in improving processes efficiencies and capitalizing on market opportunities" (p. 514). Organizations have identified knowledge management as a strategic imperative to stay competitive and to encourage employee development (Calo, 2008).

The knowledge and experience gained after long-term employment in highly complex assignments could be difficult to replicate over time. Furthermore, becoming an expert takes an inordinate amount of concentrated study and practice, opposed to an employee merely competent. Thus, Baby Boomers' exodus from the workplace could lead to organizations experiencing a shortage of skills and labor if leaders have not taken steps to employ sustainable knowledge management systems. The loss of organizational knowledge must address the potential loss of Baby Boomer employees who make up a large portion of the workforce. The Baby Boomer generation represents individuals born between 1946 and 1964 that total approximately 76 million people and potentially represent one-third of the workforce (Sasser, 2010). Generation X represents individuals born between 1965 and 1980 with Generation Y or millennial individuals born between 1981 and 1999, but both cohorts do not possess workplace competence or expertise (Meriac, Woehr, & Banister, 2010).

The problem of not sharing critical knowledge carries economic implications for corporations because of the number of Baby Boomer retirements affecting domestic and global operations. Global complexities require corporations to be flexible and adaptable to change to accommodate a changing work infrastructure. Organizational knowledge loss can adversely affect a company's ability to be competitive in a growing knowledge economy.

An aging workforce is contributing to the knowledge loss in organizations. Primarily, decreased fertility rates and higher life expectancy contribute to a shrinking and aging population (Stam, 2009). Leader and management understanding of work and knowledge behavior patterns in the development and creation of knowledge are imperative to establishing a smoother transition across multi-generational employee lines.

Statement of the Problem

The objective of this phenomenological study was to examine industrial security leaders lived experiences and perceptions regarding capturing and sharing knowledge in a United States-based Aerospace Company security organization. Global businesses are facing the challenges of an aging workforce and the loss of Baby Boomer employees if knowledge-sharing initiatives are not implemented prior to their departure (Hokanson, Sosa-Fey, & Vinaja, 2011). DeLong (2004) contended there is a loss of knowledge occurring in organizations requiring a concerted effort by leaders to create knowledge management systems. Although programs are implemented to encourage knowledge sharing, it appears there remains a reluctance to share knowledge openly among Baby Boomer employees

(O'Neill & Adya, 2007). Ball and Gotsill (2011) posited that 26% of aerospace industry employees became eligible to retire in 2008. The specific problem is the loss of critical security knowledge at a United States-based aerospace company because of the reduction of workforce, terminations, and Baby Boomer retirements occurring in key areas of the industrial security organization. Dalkir (2011) contended that reworking information because it cannot be located is costing organizations $12 million a year. A lack of trust and motivation is cited for employee reluctance to share knowledge from Baby Boomer employees (Okyere-Kwakye & Nor, 2011). Further, phenomenological researchers cannot be detached from their assumptions in describing the phenomena from the viewpoints of the participants (Groenewald, 2004).

The study originated at a United States-based aerospace company, with offices in four regions of the United States. A purposeful sample of 10 industrial security managers and 10 industrial security specialists, carefully chosen from industrial security personnel employed with the aerospace company participated in the study. The participants are subject matter experts (SME) in the government security organization. The selection criteria identified senior level security professionals responsible for multi-billion dollar programs within the United States-based aerospace company. The basis for selection of the participants used the following criteria: (a) Baby Boomer industrial security managers born between 1946 and 1964, (b) Baby Boomer industrial security specialists born between 1946 and 1964, (c) possessing a Top Secret clearance, Secret Compartmented Information (SCI) and Special Access Program (SAP), (d) eligible to retire in 5 to 10 years, and (e) work in the Northwest, Southwest, Midwest, or Eastern regional security office of the United States-based aerospace company. The management structure within the aerospace company is comprised of Level K first line managers, Level L mid-level managers, and Level M senior managers. However, the Level K managers in the industrial security organization comprised 68% of the 38 industrial security managers. Approximately 28 managers (K, L, and M) will be eligible to retire in 5 to 10 years taking with them key industrial security knowledge. Additionally, industrial security specialists with job classifications of LAHQ 1 through LAHQ 5 levels participated in the study. Level 5 industrial security personnel are subject matter experts and team leads at the aerospace company. The management and leadership experience in computing security, industrial security, and special program security could lead to a brain drain when leaders begin to leave the organization. The specialized customer knowledge could be difficult to transfer to less experienced personnel. The security knowledge and experience gained throughout an employee's tenure in a specialized industry could make it difficult to replicate across organizations, if knowledge management systems are not in place. Barachini (2009) explained that knowledge management is about learning how to motivate employees to share knowledge that can influence intellectual capital.

As Baby Boomers begin retiring, aerospace organizations could face a knowledge and capability crisis due to loss of capabilities and a shortage of younger employees to take their place (Stam, 2009). The Department of Defense (DoD) budget reductions and aerospace procurement restructuring are accelerating reductions in force (RIF), terminations, and early retirements, which can affect knowledge sharing in the workplace. Contributing factors affecting the transfer of knowledge is the underutilization of older workers (Stam, 2009). Organizational leaders who are poised to take advantage of knowledge creation and sharing strategies could gain a competitive advantage (Buckley & Giannakopoulos, 2011). Leaders face challenges of motivating managers and employees to share knowledge before Baby Boomers exit their respective companies. However, leaders and managers are responsible and accountable for developing knowledge management systems within their organizations. The researcher examined employee perspectives and lived experiences regarding the importance of knowledge sharing in an industrial security organization in support of national security objectives. Leader and management responsibility for knowledge retention is critical to creating robust knowledge management systems.

The retirement of heritage aerospace company employees representing Hughes Aircraft, McDonnell Douglas, and Rockwell International could leave a void of experienced and knowledgeable personnel in the industrial security organization. As a Level K Industrial Security Manager who is responsible for safeguarding classified information in the industrial security organization with 23 years of experience, the researcher examined if a reluctance to share knowledge can result in a skills gap among industrial security personnel.

Purpose of the Study

The reason for this qualitative phenomenological study was to examine the individual experiences and perceptions of aerospace company industrial security managers and industrial security specialists and the potential loss of knowledge and organizational readiness when Baby Boomers retire. Edmund Husserl, who focused on personal consciousness, developed the study of phenomenology. Further, a quantitative approach may or may not yield a deeper meaning and understanding of the phenomena under study (Giorgi, 2009). The study population consisted of 10 industrial security managers and 10 industrial security specialists representing the United States-based aerospace company with security offices in the Northwest, Southwest, Midwest, and Eastern regions of the country. The phenomenological study's data collection occurred through telephone and in-person interviews originating from the Huntington Beach, California aerospace company security office to industrial security offices in the Northwest, Southwest, Midwest, and Eastern regions of the country. The researcher administered 10 telephone interviews and 10 in-person interviews to evoke a robust account of the participants lived experiences (Moustakas, 1994). The government security director (see Appendix F) provided permission to use the aerospace company facility to conduct participant interviews. A purposefully selected sample population of 10 industrial security managers and 10 industrial security specialists represented the population under study.

The phenomenological study approach focused on six demographic and nine semi-structured, open-ended personal interviews posed to 10 industrial security managers and 10 industrial security specialists, holding a Top Secret clearance with SCI or SAP access, five years of work experience, and eligible to retire in 5 to 10 years. The purpose of this research was to focus on the individual experiences and perceptions regarding organizational readiness to share knowledge among industrial security leaders that will provide a foundation for further research (Moustakas, 1994). The knowledge management plan industrial security leaders have in place to capture critical knowledge amid difficult economic conditions of reduction in workforce (RIF), terminations, retirements, and program closures could affect competition among other contractor companies vying for government contracts.

Additionally, leadership identification of critical industrial security knowledge necessary to maintain a competitive advantage and operational efficiency emerged during the participant interviews. The results of the phenomenological study provided leadership insight into how organizational competitiveness and sustainment occurs during large-scale retirements, or is part of a reduction in force. The phenomenological data analysis occurred through an adapted van Kamm technique (Moustakas, 1994).

Significance of the Study

The inability to capture and share knowledge
among industrial security employees contributes to a
knowledge gap that can affect an organization's
competitive advantage. The researcher examined an
aging workforce at a global aerospace corporation
and the increased complexities of technically
challenging tasks. The research study added to the
existing knowledge management theory by
addressing knowledge creation and knowledge
sharing opportunities and strategies within an
industrial security organization. Conducting the study
revealed the potential loss of knowledge among
industrial security employees within the S&FP
organization. Furthermore, demographic data suggest
a loss of approximately 52% of the S&FP security
personnel eligible to retire in the next 5 to 10 years
(as of date of this study; 2014).

This phenomenological study provided
awareness into the problem of departing knowledge
workers, the serious effect lost knowledge has on the
company, and the effect knowledge loss can have on
remaining employees tasked with filling the gaps of

departed knowledge workers. Organizational knowledge creation grounded on employment conditions where creative and innovative work on ideas is valued, and a system is in place for selecting ideas that can be further developed (van Aalst, 2009). Results of the research study will benefit researchers, leaders, and practitioners by providing insight into knowledge management during a generational transition to leadership and non-leadership positions. Such insight can shape the leaders' perception of an organizations willingness to acknowledge the possibility of knowledge loss when knowledge workers depart from the organization. Additionally, the results assess leadership perspectives relative to capturing Baby Boomer knowledge in restructuring and producing more with less (Trugman-Nikol, 2011). The phenomenological study helped leaders understand the perceived reluctance of industrial security managers and security specialists to share their knowledge, skills, and experiences in an industrial security organization. Furthermore, industrial security leader interest in employee perceptions prompted them to create and develop knowledge management systems within the industrial security organization, which is comprised of both DoD and special programs security professionals.

Significance of the Study to Leadership.

Leaders and managers are in a position to address which forms of knowledge they will retain or discard. However, organizational productivity hinges on worker willingness to share knowledge (Barachini, 2009). Additionally, contrasting value systems of cross-generational employees, such as Baby Boomers and industrial security non-managers, could add to the existing knowledge management literature. The increased attrition rates at many organizations and older employees working past their retirement age can pose strategic challenges for leaders and managers. The recession of 2008 caused older workers to postpone retirements, electing to wait for the U.S. economy to rebound (Toossi, 2012). The percentage of older workers aged 55 or older is growing faster than any other group, with an expectation to live and work longer than the past generation (GAO, 2008). The results of the interpretive phenomenological study contributed to the fields of organizational leadership and knowledge management. From a knowledge management perspective, the risk of aging focuses attention on underutilized older employees and the loss of knowledge (Stam, 2009). The recognition and better utilization of older employees will challenge leaders in the coming years (Stam, 2009). The loss of knowledge is attributed to large numbers of experienced workers retiring, taking with them knowledge, skills, and attitudes (Stam, 2009). The effective transfer of knowledge from older to younger generational employees will challenge leaders and in the coming years.

This research study contributed to existing knowledge management theories by helping leaders develop and implement knowledge management strategies to help minimize the effect of knowledge loss in an industrial security organization and to sustain a competitive advantage. This research study helped leaders understand the perceived reluctance of industrial security managers and team leads to participate in knowledge sharing activities in an industrial security organization. Leaders and managers face the challenge of making knowledge management part of the business strategy through communication and employee education.

Peter Drucker emphasized the importance of the shift to knowledge workers in the identification of tasks that contributed to knowledge worker productivity gains in all industries. Knowledge workers are task oriented, in comparison to manual workers who are oriented by the work (Drucker, 1999). Focusing on creating knowledge workers could change the way worker task performance occurs in aerospace organizations past and present. The shift to knowledge workers emphasizes the importance placed on leaders to identify knowledge management systems designed to create a culture of sharing across organizations.

The research study focused on the aerospace industry; however, these findings correlate to other industries connected with national security related issues because the current research study could identify organizational barriers that industrial security leaders have to overcome to create meaningful change. In the security industry, leaders face challenges of managing complex technical knowledge and processes requiring documentation and work sharing among personnel. The research study provided industrial security leaders and non-managers with alternative methods and strategies for transferring knowledge to a multi-generational workforce. Leaders and managers must identify management strategies of multi-generational employees in the development of knowledge creation and knowledge sharing opportunities. Toossi (2009) stated, "In 2018, Baby Boomers will be between 54 and 72, and they will be past their strongest years of attachment to the labor market" (p. 39). In contrast, human resources personnel are working to accommodate shifting demographics and coexistence of a multi-generational workforce. The study provided a better understanding of how leadership relates to inspiring and motivating employees to create and share knowledge.

Nature of the Study.

This phenomenological study was appropriate because the researcher's objective was to examine the lived experiences and perceptions of aerospace company industrial security managers and industrial security specialists and the potential loss of knowledge and organizational readiness when Baby Boomers retire. A quantitative study was not appropriate because the study is not theory based (Shank, 2006). More important, a quantitative approach contradicts the participant's involvement in providing a textural description of thoughts, feelings, examples, ideas, and situations that comprise their experiences (Moustakas, 1994).

A qualitative research method allows participants to answer research questions with detailed descriptions, which is essential to the study (Jamerson, 2009). Qualitative researchers rely on social science as the mechanism for observing subject interaction. A phenomenological technique was the best approach in exploring the research questions regarding organizational readiness to share knowledge among industrial security professionals when Baby Boomers depart. The phenomenological researcher examines and describes participant experiences as it relates to the phenomenon (Creswell, 2012). According to Shank (2006), qualitative inquiry revolves around three tenets: the researcher matters, inquiry leading to understanding, and inquiry leading to new ways of observing the world around us.

The exploration of knowledge sharing in an aerospace corporation consisted of six demographic questions, nine semi-structured questions; digitally recorded, open-ended telephone, and in-person interviews. The participants met the following criteria: (a) 10 Baby Boomer industrial security managers born between 1946 and 1964; (b) 10 Baby Boomer industrial security specialists born between 1946 and 1964; (c) holding a Top Secret clearance, Secret Compartmented Information (SCI) and Special Access Program (SAP) access; (d) eligible to retire in 5 to 10 years; and (e) work in the Northwest, Southwest, Midwest, or Eastern regional security office of a United States-based aerospace company.

The phenomenological study is important to understanding the reluctance of industrial security managers and security specialists to share knowledge and organizational readiness when employees depart the organization. This study explored employee perceptions and lived experiences regarding organizational readiness to share knowledge when

Baby Boomers depart. The phenomenological method described and explored the lived experiences of the participants instead of evaluating the experiences (Allah, 2011). In contrast, lack of reflection on individuals' experiences take for granted the extraordinary experiences observed by pausing and reflecting on the phenomenon (Van Manen, 2014). The population consisted of 10 industrial security managers and 10 industrial security specialists representing a United States-based aerospace company with security offices located in the Northwest, Southwest, Midwest, and Eastern regions of the country. The phenomenological study design consisted of six demographic, nine semi-structured, open-ended telephone, and in-person interview questions administered to 20 industrial security personnel to understand organizational readiness when security personnel begin to retire and their reluctance to share knowledge in an industrial security organization.

Furthermore, six demographic and nine semi-structured, open-ended interview questions were administered in-person, and by telephone and digitally recorded to ensure each participant is queried by an identical set of questions on the same topic to preserve comparability across interviews. The phenomenological study provided rich information about the social process in the industrial security arena. Giorgi (2009) posited the researcher should understand the psychological and social occurrences from research experiences of study participants. In contrast, an ethnographic study was not conducive to this study because of the inordinate amount of time necessary to observe participants in the profession. Moustakas (1994) stated, "In phenomenological investigation the researcher has a personal interest in whatever he or she seeks to know; the researcher is intimately connected with the phenomenon" (p. 59). The researcher explored and interpreted participant responses to social actions, where a subjective meaning yields rich and insightful patterns of interpretation for the researcher. This phenomenological study methodology explored knowledge sharing experiences within the industrial security organization. The researcher examined industrial security leader reluctance to share knowledge among industrial security personnel and organizational readiness in response to employee retirements, layoffs, and terminations. The researcher observed the social relationship between manager and worker as an opportunity to develop knowledge management systems and methods for sustaining a competitive advantage.

Detailed personal evaluations and experiences, collected through six demographic and nine semi-structured, open-ended telephone, and in-person were digitally recorded and transcribed interviews encompassed the data collection stage of the study.

Prior to the interview, the researcher advised participants that detailed and reflective interviews are welcomed (Irvine, 2011). There was a steady substitution of face-to-face interviewing with telephone interviewing as a data collection method (Holbrook, Green, & Krosnick, 2003). The researcher administered 15 semi-structured, open-ended telephone, and in-person interview questions to 20 industrial security participants. Participants received the 15 research questions prior to the main in-person and telephone interviews. The participants had time to absorb the nine content and six demographic related research questions prior to the scheduled interview.

The researcher was cognizant of the 1-hour use of the participant's personal time to conduct the interview to obtain a revelatory description of their lived experiences (Giorgi, 2009). The analysis, coding, interpretation, and categorization of the nine semi-structured and six demographic open-ended interview responses occurred during the data collection phase. The researcher incorporated in-person interviews to ensure data collection and analysis is robust and revealing. Shank (2006) contended that face-to-face interviews are an option to pursue when feasible; however, telephone interviews can be an adequate substitute. Telephone interviews are flexible and as reliable as face-to-face interviews, with half the cost (Neuman, 2003). The technological capabilities that telephone interviewing possess make it comparable with face-to-face interviewing (Quinn, Gutek, & Walsh, 1980).

To facilitate effective telephone interviews, the researcher established a common ground with each participant early in the interview process to help draw out responses (Irvine, 2011). During the interview, the researcher's objective was to obtain a description of the experience each research participant has lived through (Giorgi, 2009). The researcher's solicitation script identified the nature of the study and research participant guidelines. More important, telephone interviewing strengths are similar to face-to-face interviews, and could improve the quality of the data collected (Glogowska, Young, & Lockyer, 2011). Further, the researcher created a climate of trust to ensure each participant answers each question openly and honestly (Moustakas, 1994).

Overview of the Research Method

A phenomenological method was suitable for this qualitative study because the participant's individual experiences and perceptions reveal personal observations of the phenomenon under study. A purposeful sample of 10 industrial security managers and 10 industrial security specialists were chosen for this study within the aerospace company security organization. The following criteria was required for the inclusion of security managers and industrial security specialists as participants in this study: (a) 10 Baby Boomer industrial security managers born between 1946 and 1964; (b) 10 Baby

Boomer industrial security specialists born between 1946 and 1964; (c) holding a Top Secret clearance, Secret Compartmented Information (SCI) and Special Access Program (SAP) access; (d) eligible to retire in 5 to 10 years; and (e) work in the Northwest, Southwest, Midwest, or Eastern regional security office of a United States-based aerospace company.

Industrial security managers and industrial security specialists Level 5 personnel who are Generation X and Y employees did not participate in this study. The study focused on industrial security personnel born between 1946 and 1964 and eligible to retire in 5 to 10 years. A solicitation script was used to identify purposefully selected industrial security managers and industrial security specialists Level 5 personnel. The study focused on industrial security personnel born between 1946 and 1964 and eligible to retire in 5 to 10 years. The phenomenological researcher explored the lived experiences and perceptions of industrial security personnel regarding organizational readiness when Baby Boomers begin to retire from industrial security positions. Baby Boomer industrial security managers and industrial security specialists purposefully selected and included in the study to ascertain organizational readiness when Baby Boomers retire and to address security personnel who are reluctant to share knowledge. The phenomenological study method is a process where Baby Boomer industrial security managers and industrial security specialists respond to structured, open-ended interview questions.

Overview of the Design Appropriateness.

This interpretive phenomenological study is the most appropriate method for solicitation of knowledge experts in the industrial security profession. As Van Manen (2014) stated, "Generally, the social sciences such as sociology, psychology, and ethnography aim at explanation, while phenomenology aims at description and interpretation" (p. 43). The researcher acts in a participant-observer role by becoming part of the culture having the ability to describe the activity and event in greater detail. As a research tool, the phenomenological study technique is essential for describing, analyzing, and interpreting industrial security personnel behavior and beliefs in the interpretation of the structured interview questions. The participant responses were anonymous, with controlled feedback, making the phenomenological study method a useful and appropriate research method. This phenomenological study concentrated on knowledge sharing between industrial security managers, industrial security specialists, and multi-generational employees. The phenomenological design facilitated open discussion by study participants to understand organizational readiness better when Baby Boomers begin to retire (Allah, 2011).

Pilot Study.

The researcher provided a pilot study that evaluates performance characteristics and capabilities of study designs, measurements, procedures, selection methods, and strategies that are representative of a larger study (Moore, Carter, Nietert, & Stewart, 2011). This is a necessary step to clarifying and ensuring the reliability and accuracy of the research tool. A pilot study contributed to the analysis through testing out components like sample size estimation, randomization, and accuracy (Arain,

Campbell, Cooper, & Lancaster, 2010). The pilot study identified weakness in the design and instrumentation prior to disseminating the research questions. The pilot study deployment offered an exploration of the study to identify logistical problems (Duma, Khanyile, & Daniels, 2009).

The pilot study added value and credibility to the study by validating the research questions before moving on to the main study (Duma et al., 2009). A pilot study was administered to three Baby Boomer industrial security managers adhering to the following criteria: (a) 10 Baby Boomer industrial security managers born between 1946 and 1964; (b) 10 Baby Boomer industrial security specialists born between 1946 and 1964; (c) holding a Top Secret clearance, Secret Compartmented Information (SCI) and Special Access Program (SAP) access; (d) eligible to retire in 5 to 10 years; and (e) work in the Northwest, Southwest, Midwest, or Eastern regional security office of a United States-based aerospace company. The three participants, purposefully selected to participate in the pilot study, provided consistent observations. Pilot study participants received an informed consent agreement form (see Appendix C) that participants must be read, sign, and return to the researcher.

The purposeful sample pilot study was administered face-to-face to three industrial security managers representing a United States-based aerospace company with offices in the Southwest, Northwest, Midwest, and Eastern regions of the country. The three industrial security managers selected using the Enterprise Plant Security System (EPSS) database recognizing their expertise and managerial background (Oliver, 2010). The EPSS database is a central repository for all industrial security and customer related information. The purposeful sample selection process entails identification of all Baby Boomer industrial security managers by the following criteria: Job Title, United States Aerospace Electronic Messaging Service (USAEMS), Name, Work City, Work State, Service Year, Clearance, SAP, and SCI.

The three pilot study industrial security managers did not participate in the personal interviews with the 20 industrial security managers and industrial security specialists representing security offices located in the Northwest, Southwest,

Midwest, and Eastern regions. The three industrial security managers reviewed six demographic and nine semi-structured, open-ended interview questions for clarity and accuracy to increase the reliability of the interview questions. Data analysis from the pilot study occurred before administering the interview questions to the purposely-selected 20 Baby Boomer industrial security managers and industrial security specialists.

The phenomenological study explores the knowledge creation and sharing methods within the industrial security organization. Prior to beginning the main study, the researcher obtained permissions from the aerospace company, industrial security director, and the study participants. Each research study participant signed an informed consent form, prior to initiating the main study (see Appendix C). The researcher provided the informed consent form to each study participant through company e-mail. Upon completion of the informed consent form, the participants mailed the completed document to the researcher. The participants were advised of the withdrawal procedure, with no penalty for withdrawing before, during or after the administration of the study begins. If and when a participant withdrew from the study, all of the research documentation is destroyed immediately. The researcher will delete all electronic files, and all hard copy information. Any participants who may have been removed from the study were not part of the data analysis. When the researcher received the informed consent forms, he scheduled in-person and telephone interviews with participants. The researcher used a spreadsheet to log e-mail delivery of the interview questions to the 20 participants. Each participant's interview questions were alpha-numerically coded to ensure confidentiality during distribution.

The target population of 10 industrial security managers and 10 industrial security specialists chosen using a purposeful sampling method obtained from personally identified information (PII) of Baby Boomer industrial security managers and security specialists obtained from the EPSS database repository. The 20 industrial security employees participated in answering six demographic and nine semi-structured, open-ended interview questions. The 10 industrial security managers and security specialists chosen from the target population of 40 industrial security managers and 550 security specialists using the EPSS database repository. The phenomenological study relied on the data collected from six demographic and nine semi-structured, open-ended participant interview responses to describe the phenomenon under study from the participant's experience as security professionals. Visual observation of the participants was not possible because of the physical work location and lack of proximity of the study participants whom were located in various regions of the country.

The researcher could not see non-verbal behavioral mannerisms during the telephone interview exchange. The six demographic and nine semi-structured, open-ended interview questions were designed to capture qualitative data in searching for themes and patterns in developing relationships. In comparison to other qualitative research methods, the telephone interview questions are necessary when participants in a study are geographically unable to meet in person. Other qualitative research methods, such as direct observation, could reveal behavioral changes and were included in the research study. The proximity of the participants located in various regions of the country made the majority of the telephone interviews a viable instrument for this study.

Seven of the 20 interview questions were administered in-person to encourage a comprehensive account of the participant's lived experiences within the security organization (Moustakas, 1994). Qualitative data was collected and recorded using ATLAS.ti 7, a database software analysis tool, to organize, record, code, and analyze data reported by participants. The researcher's objective was to examine organizational readiness to capture and share knowledge among industrial security personnel. The selection of the phenomenological methodology was based on the researcher's intimate knowledge and experience as a 28-year employee of the aerospace company with 23 years' experience in industrial security. An ethnographic study could require prolonged observational fieldwork, with the researcher incurring additional cost and jeopardizing the completion of the study. A grounded theory was not a suitable methodology, because it builds a theory from the ground up, allowing the data to guide the growth and development of the theory (Shank, 2006).

Research Questions.

Qualitative research questions led the researcher to obtaining a meaningful understanding of the phenomenon. The research questions explored the practices and perceptions of industrial security managers and security specialists toward organizational readiness when Baby Boomer security employees depart the industrial security organization. More important, the research questions yielded additional knowledge transfer methodologies within an aerospace organization tasked with protecting national security. The reason for this interpretive phenomenological research study was to examine the individual experiences and perceptions of industrial security employees tasked with sharing knowledge and developing knowledge management systems in an industrial security organization. The phenomenological research questions emphasized individual experiences and perceptions of industrial security professionals regarding organizational readiness when Baby Boomers begin to retire and a willingness to share knowledge among security personnel. By examining organizational leader readiness to address Baby Boomer retirements and knowledge sharing, this study focused on the primary question: How are industrial security leaders and security specialists able to sustain a competitive advantage when industrial security personnel leave the organization with experience, knowledge, and skills? The main research questions of this study focused on manager and non-manager perceptions and experiences toward knowledge sharing in an industrial security organization:

RQ1: What are the lived experiences of industrial security managers transferring knowledge from more senior employees to newer employees?

RQ1 was central to understanding the potential effect to national security if knowledge does not transfer from senior employees to newer employees. Industrial security managers are responsible for cultivating knowledge sharing in a budget-constrained environment. Security leaders must be creative and innovative in developing knowledge transfer opportunities among security personnel. The skills gap among retirement eligible Baby Boomer employees could widen if security leaders ignore the warning signs. When leaders fail to incorporate knowledge sharing as a strategic objective for the company and security organization, the competitive advantage is threatened.

RQ2: What are the lived experiences of industrial security specialists transferring knowledge from more senior employees to newer employees?

RQ2 yielded meaningful knowledge transfer opportunities from older employee to multi-generational employees. The transfer of knowledge is important to organizations in sustaining a competitive advantage amid DoD budget reductions because of difficult economic conditions. Industrial security specialists are in a position to address knowledge transfer methods such as best practices, creating a learning organization, improved processes, and cross-functional support. Industrial security specialists, considered subject matter experts, are responsible for managing multi-million-dollar defense programs. The industrial security subject matter experts rely on tacit knowledge, which is described as knowledge developed from experience and action, difficult to describe, and shared through discussion and common experiences (Kothari, Bickford, Edwards, Dobbins, & Meyer, 2011). The subject matter experts are in lead positions responsible for delivering security services across organizational boundaries.

Additionally, industrial security employee perception and experiences of knowledge sharing activities occurring in the security organization yielded important information toward the creation and deployment of knowledge sharing and learning among security personnel. Security leaders who do not cultivate a sharing and learning environment toward championing a knowledge management approach could face obstacles if leaders do not engage, reward, or communicate with employees (O'Dell & Hubert, 2011). Leaders and managers who hoarded knowledge will face difficulty in changing behaviors of less experienced and unmotivated employees. RQ2 provided the researcher with first-hand observations of factors that could contribute to effective knowledge sharing.

RQ3: What lived experiences prevent sharing industrial security knowledge at the aerospace company?

In contrast, RQ3 industrial security leaders and managers who do not foster a knowledge sharing culture within their organization face questionable strategic goals and objectives. Industrial security personnel responded to RQ3 about the factors not associated with knowledge sharing in their organization. Participant responses provided leaders with recommendations toward creating and/or improving knowledge sharing opportunities in an industrial security organization. This question identified security leaders who lack necessary skills and abilities to create knowledge sharing opportunities.

RQ4: What knowledge management strategies are used to ensure industrial security knowledge transfers from retiring senior employees to newer employees?

RQ4 focused on the impending retirement of senior security employees and the importance of having a robust knowledge management system in place that will identify departing employees who leave with tacit knowledge after years of working in sensitive positions in the safeguarding of classified information critical to national security. RQ4 provided participant perspectives on organizational strategies designed to transfer knowledge from retiring employee to newer employees. Therefore, RQ4 provides a structure for the creation of knowledge management systems necessary to fill the skill gaps from departing older workers to remaining multi-generational employees. Security leaders and specialists possess critical security knowledge transferrable to younger employees to sustain a competitive advantage among similar aerospace companies. The researcher examined the theoretical framework associated with knowledge management and motivation for capturing and sharing knowledge between managers and industrial security employees of the United States-based aerospace company.

Conceptual Framework.

The conceptual framework focuses on three main theories: knowledge management, social exchange, and expectancy theories. Peter Drucker's groundbreaking research on the emergence of knowledge workers helped develop the discipline of promoting the leveraging, creation, and sharing of organizational knowledge. Drucker (1999) coined the phrase, *knowledge worker*, where the responsibility for their productivity fell on themselves. The Baby Boomer exodus is promoting the need to create and share knowledge before knowledge walks out the door. Organizations are making knowledge management a strategic initiative to sustain a competitive advantage. Knowledge workers were concerned with what the task was, opposed to manual labor worker concern with where the task was provided (or accomplished).

Organizational assets originate in the knowledge resident in the minds of employees, which can be susceptible to loss when employees depart from the organization (Durst & Wilhelm, 2011). The emergence of a knowledge economy is important to an organization's strategy of achieving a sustained competitive advantage. Corporations rely on a dynamic management approach toward the creation of knowledge in social interactions (Nonaka & Nishiguchi, 2001). Development of organizational strategies to capture and retain knowledge from older workers is critical to the effective transferring of knowledge to other employees in the corporation (Calo, 2008).

Organizational strategy develops by drawing on the collective knowledge of workers to meet goals and objectives of the corporation. Organizational leaders who embrace knowledge management understand the need for a systemic and comprehensive plan of the competencies it intends to develop (Pasher & Ronen, 2011). Furthermore, the promotion of a shared culture free of the command and control leadership style can lead to successful knowledge management systems.

An authoritarian and hierarchical management style is counterproductive to a knowledge management culture that emphasizes innovation. An open style of leadership has employees taking on

more responsibility, creating, and innovating new
knowledge (Pasher & Ronen, 2011). A key
component within knowledge management systems is
knowledge sharing, which saves the company time
and resources and eliminates rework. Leaders are
responsible for creating a knowledge sharing culture
by influencing behavioral norms and practices of their
employees (Pasher & Ronen, 2011). From an
organizational perspective, knowledge is a strategic
resource leveraged through the sharing and reuse of
knowledge. Knowledge transfer occurs when best
practices toward becoming a learning organization
with the capability of inspiring a shared vision takes
place (English & Baker, 2006). Organizational
workers can benefit from sharing knowledge through
visibility, recognition, and advancement opportunities.
Managers who do not embrace knowledge sharing
can deter workers from acknowledging organizational
benefits from knowledge sharing.

Furthermore, Wysocki's (2009) Baby Boomer
exodus study sought to build on previous literature in
the field of knowledge management by overcoming
impending retirement and brain drain of Baby
Boomers as leaders and to document and store

critical organizational knowledge. The identification of the leader, manager, and employee influencing factors emerged as knowledge transfer opportunities. Another conceptual framework of this study examined a multi-theoretical model using Peter Blau's (1964/2008) social exchange theory and Henry Vroom's (1964) expectancy theory. The model offers an explanation as to why individuals contribute valuable knowledge that will assist others. Blau's seminal work describes the social exchange and reciprocity between worker and manager. Blau posited that a social exchange occurs when one person does another a favor, with the expectation of a future return (Blau, 1964/2008). Leaders face the challenge of motivating individuals to share knowledge during difficult economic conditions where jobs are becoming scarce and cooperative behavior is not recognized or rewarded by the organization.

Blau (1964/2008) posited that social exchanges are actions by individuals motivated by their expected return. The multi-theoretical model in Figure 1 represents a single, complex system, depicting the flow of knowledge *into* and *out of* the system to other individuals (Watson & Hewett, 2006).

Social Exchange Theory Model

Valuable Knowledge Contributed INTO the System

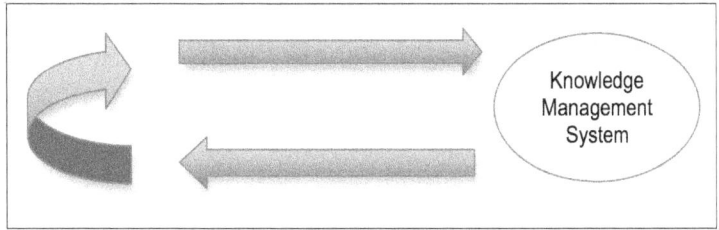

Expectancy Theory Model

Figure 1. Building an Effective Knowledge Transfer System.[1]

Therefore, the motivation for sharing knowledge emphasizes the benefit from the knowledge submitted by others (Watson & Hewett, 2006). Willis (2010) provided a study that emphasized Blau's social exchange theory to help understand effects of turnover, retention, and motivation in a public child welfare agency. Additionally, in this study workers perceived that organizational leaders appreciate and fairly compensate employees based on knowledge, experience, and job performance that can lead to

---

[1] *Adapted from "A Multi-Theoretical Model of Knowledge Transfer in Organizations: Determinants of Knowledge Contribution and Knowledge Reuse (Watson & Hewett, 2006).*

positive behavior (Willis, 2010). In this study, public
child welfare workers, who believed their expectations
failed to be met, showed lower levels of job
involvement, consistent with Blau's expectancy theory
(Willis, 2010). Social exchange theorists explained
that individual behavior is influenced by the need to
reduce undesirable occurrences and increase
constructive occurrences (Willis, 2010). The
integration of the social exchange theory in this study
provided a basic understanding of the structure of the
interaction between caseworker, supervisor, and
coworker (Willis, 2010).

Blau's social exchange theory is pertinent to
this study because it addresses intangible social costs
and benefits influenced by leaders and managers.
The social exchange theory identifies the reward and
exchange process with emphasis on trust to stimulate
cooperation and creation of goodwill (Blau,
1964/2008). The social exchange theory provides
leaders with an opportunity to gain influence from
demonstrations of expertise and loyalty (Yukl, 2010).
Leaders who have the ability to create value-added
benefits can influence knowledge sharing in
organizations. Sharing knowledge is not an official

task of leaders, but it is necessary to keep the company in a competitive position (DeLong, 2004). Leaders who can foster a culture where individuals are encouraged to create and share new knowledge will gain a competitive advantage (Rai, 2011). A positive social exchange occurs when employees perceive the reward they gain is less than the cost they invest, and they stop the transaction (Blau, 1964/2008). With declining organizational budgets, leaders and managers face challenges with finding ways to incentivize individuals to share knowledge. This research compliments previous research by addressing knowledge sharing among personnel of an aerospace company in an industrial security organization. Leader and employee perspectives offer viewpoints during difficult economic conditions, where knowledge sharing may not be occurring. Previous research addressed the knowledge drain occurring in organizations because of Baby Boomer retirements. In comparison, Baby Boomer retirements, layoffs, and redeployments to other areas of the aerospace company can build on prior research.

Vroom's expectancy theory suggested that individuals are motivated to execute when they receive reward for completing the assigned task

(Watson & Hewett, 2006). Leaders face financial

challenges with reduced budgets that impede reward

and recognition opportunities for worker contributions.

Innovative and creative leaders find ways to motivate

and encourage individuals to collaborate in

knowledge sharing opportunities. Furthermore,

Vroom's expectancy theory examined the complex

relationship between social motivation and work. The

following three perceptions and beliefs are central to

Vroom's theory: (a) the belief that some effort will lead

to achieving the desired outcome, (b) achieving the

outcome will lead to receiving something, and (c) the

value of achieving the outcome (Watson & Hewett,

2006, p. 152). Turcan's (2010) study emphasized

Vroom's expectancy theory in determining faculty

motivation using the blackboard tools that were

available to classroom instructors. Vroom's

expectancy theory, rigorously tested in business and

industry settings as applied in motivational studies

(Turcan, 2010). The multi-theoretical model

describes the stream of knowledge that flows into the

system and the knowledge that is reused from the

system (Watson & Hewett, 2006). With improved

training individuals are more likely to achieve outcomes critical to improving an organization's knowledge sharing culture.

The inclusion of the knowledge management theory to this study emphasizes the need for organizations to create comprehensive knowledge management systems prior to Baby Boomer exodus. The addition of knowledge management as a strategic imperative acknowledges the importance placed on organizations for developing systems to manage knowledge. Knowledge management is a method for gathering and distributing information used to support tasks and leadership decisions toward sustaining a competitive advantage. The perceived reluctance of industrial security managers to share knowledge with multi-generational individuals promoted the importance of including Vroom's expectancy theory into this study. The expectancy theory compliments this study through the multi-theoretical approach toward building an effective knowledge management system. The introduction of valuable knowledge into the system through the generation, representation, storage, access, and transfer of knowledge helps to explain why individuals willingly provide useful knowledge for another person's benefit (Watson & Hewett, 2006). The social exchange theory, popularized by Blau, provided a better understanding of individual behavior and other issues that obstructed or enabled knowledge sharing in organizations. The social exchange theory was important to this phenomenological study, because it addresses motivational factors that influence individuals to share their knowledge toward creating robust knowledge management systems.

Definition of Terms

The terms and definitions listed below clarify meaning of key areas within the phenomenological research study. The definitions below are associated with the theoretical framework of the phenomenological study.

Baby Boomers: The largest group of knowledge workers born between the years 1946 and 1964 (Toossi, 2005).

Communities of Practice: A community of practice (CoP) occurs when groups of individuals with similar concerns about a problem expands their knowledge through group interaction (Krishnaveni & Sujatha, 2012).

Expectancy Theory: Expectancy is a belief that an action will be followed by some outcome (Vroom, 1964).

Explicit Knowledge: Becerra-Fernandez et al. (2004) stated, "Explicit knowledge refers to knowledge that has been expressed into words and numbers" (p. 19).

Generation X: Individual birth's between 1965 and 1976, a reduction in the number of births occurred and led to a smaller population referred to as baby bust or Generation X workers who will be between 25 to 54 years of age from 2004 to 2014 (Toossi, 2005).

Generation Y: Comprised of children born to baby boom generation after 1976 and until 2001 (Toossi, 2005).

Knowledge Management System: Factors to be mindful of when designing a knowledge management system are (a) provide basis for valuation, (b) keep management focused upon strategic imperatives, and (c) to validate investments (Anantatmula, 2009).

Knowledge worker: The hiring of knowledge workers, which are jobs that involve exchanging information, products, or services makeup the majority of work performed in the United States (Galagan, 2010).

Leader-Member Exchange Theory: George Graen's leader-member exchange theory (LMX) is an important construct to understanding the role of leaders toward influencing knowledge sharing across organizational boundaries (Schermerhorn et al., 2003).

Social Exchange Theory: Research findings suggested that positive actions toward employees contributed to high quality exchange relationships (Settoon, Bennett, & Liden, 1996).

Tacit Knowledge: Personal knowledge that is specific to a situation, and difficult to validate and disseminate (Nonaka & Takeuchi, 1995).

Transactional Leadership: Transactional leaders obtain follower compliance through an exchange process, void of enthusiasm to completion of their tasks (Yukl, 2010).

Transformational Leadership: Transformational leaders ask followers to forego their self-interest for the good of the group, organization or society (Bass, 1990).

Assumptions

Multiple assumptions exist regarding this research study. The overall assumption of the phenomenological research study was that creating and sharing of knowledge between industrial security managers and employees does occur in a large-scale global aerospace company. The second assumption is any knowledge sharing occurring in an aerospace company can sustain a competitive advantage. The third assumption is this research study yielded strategies for successful implementation and deployment of a robust knowledge management system. The fourth assumption is the semi-structured, open-ended interview questions yielded enough data to convince security leaders to create knowledge management systems.

The fifth assumption is that Baby Boomers and multi-generational employees will respond to the study protocols openly and honestly. The interview questions designed to solicit critical information specific to identifying knowledge sharing gaps is a sixth assumption. A seventh assumption is confidentiality led to truthful responses to the semi-structured, open-ended interview questions. This assumption influenced researcher interpretation of participant interview responses. A final assumption was the phenomenological study was the most viable method for the research topic to obtain expert opinions, perceptions, and lived experiences toward the identification of obstacles to creating and sharing knowledge between Baby Boomer industrial security managers and multi-generational industrial security employees. This assumption influenced the researcher to ignore and miss knowledge creating and sharing activities occurring within an industrial security organization. The phenomenological study's generalizability to other industries, both domestically and globally and who have impending Baby Boomer retirements and do not foster an organizational readiness to share knowledge. The small sample size of 20 industrial security participants does not diminish from generalizing the study to industries that have not taken appropriate steps toward implementing knowledge management systems. The anticipated study results provided rich content from a single knowledgeable participant useful to people outside of industrial security (Given, 2008).

Scope and Limitations

The range of this research study was comprised of Baby Boomers and multi-generational industrial security professionals from a United States-based aerospace company with offices in the Northwest, Southwest, Midwest, and Eastern regions of the United States. The phenomenological research focused on management strategies, knowledge transfer procedures, and techniques to improve knowledge creation and sharing among industrial security manager and multi-generational employees in an industrial security organization. A research limitation was confining the research to the industrial security organization of the United States-based aerospace company and not including the entire population of the Industrial Security and Fire Protection organization of 1,392 employees.

Another study limitation was the lack of a comparison between male and female industrial security managers participating in knowledge creation and sharing activities. Another limitation was that Baby Boomers and multi-generational employees did not have preconceived ideas or notions when responding to the semi-structured, open-ended interview questions. Industrial security personnel could be reluctant to share personal perspectives with the researcher or be unclear of the nature of the research. The phenomenological study focus was private sector specific, which could limit the study's effectiveness. Furthermore, analysis was required from public sector security organizations similar in size and scope. However, research indicated public sector organizations were lagging behind the private sector in understanding the benefits of knowledge management (Arora, 2011). Expanding the study to decision-makers interested in creating an understanding of the risk of the loss of knowledge was another research objective. The study was limited to a defense industrial security business unit, omitting the commercial aircraft employees, which numbers 80,000 employees or half of the employee population of the United States-based aerospace company. A final limitation of the study was the omission of senior leaders located internationally, which may have yielded global knowledge creation and sharing perspectives germane to the study. The global complexities and competition in the defense and commercial aircraft divisions require qualified and knowledgeable leaders. The silo effect was apparent in the aerospace area, where security disciplines at the site, DoD, and special program arenas do not intermingle, making the transfer of knowledge difficult. Hislop (2009) described the difficulty of managing knowledge, however, leaders were in a position of power to shape the way staff use, create, and share knowledge. The researcher encountered delimitations affecting this study in the following section.

Delimitations

The researcher imposed delimitations of the phenomenological population of 20 industrial security managers and industrial security specialists limited the research to aerospace related companies only. The delimitations of the results and recommendations of this study represented one aerospace company selected for this research while making it difficult to generalize. The small study population of 20 industrial security professionals was limited to one aerospace company that delivers industrial security services to the following: special access programs, intelligence, and department of defense environments. One other delimitation was restricting the pilot study population of three industrial security managers to the Southwest region of the United States-based aerospace company instead of including participants from each of the four regions of the aerospace company. The researcher's selection of the phenomenological study while foregoing other methods delimited the study.

Summary

Chapter 1 provided the basis for the research study by describing the impending problem of knowledge sharing in an industrial security organization from Baby Boomers to multi-generational employees. The research addresses a macro observation of knowledge management within the industrial security organization. Demographic changes were effecting organizations in the loss of Baby Boomers to retirement, reduction in force, and attrition. An essential strategy for corporations was to develop comprehensive knowledge management systems designed to capture critical knowledge. Dalkir (2011) posited, "knowledge management is the deliberate and systematic coordination of an organization's people, technology, processes, and organizational structure in order to add value through reuse and innovation" (p. 4). The prevalence of knowledge workers had reshaped the role of managers in development and cultivation of their employees. Organizations faced challenges to transfer knowledge from highly skilled and qualified personnel to less qualified multi-generational employees. A lack of urgency among security managers contributed to the lack of robust knowledge management systems in organizations.

The intent of the study was to identify strategies for the successful transfer of knowledge in an industrial security organization. Chapter 1 identified the challenges facing industrial security managers and security specialists with sharing knowledge with a multi-generational workforce. The contrasting value systems between Baby Boomers and multi-generational employees offered insight into improving contributions to the advancement of knowledge. A phenomenological technique provided participant experience and perceptions reinforcing the research methodology to capture and retain qualitative data. The research questions were created to solicit feedback from industrial security managers and security specialists responsible for transferring knowledge to multi-generational employees. From a theoretical perspective, knowledge management, Blau's social exchange theory, and Vroom's expectancy theory provided a conceptual framework of the study. Eight assumptions were identified that could affect the study results. Study limitations were identified to ensure future research takes into account public and private industries. Study delimitations identified potential weaknesses of the study requiring further research.

Organizations implement knowledge management programs to cultivate knowledge sharing among employees. The loss of organizational knowledge can affect a company's competitive advantage if knowledge management systems may not be in place. Leaders and managers are in a position to assess knowledge gaps or knowledge risks if individuals retired, terminated, and reduction in force from the organization. The risk of not having knowledge management systems in place limits organizations from promoting knowledge sharing practices (O'Dell & Hubert, 2011). The United States-based aerospace company industrial security organization was under study to address the four research questions designed to solicit perceptions and lived experiences of knowledge sharing among security managers.

A phenomenological study method was employed to narrate the story and illustrated the lived

experiences of the industrial security employees for
common themes and trends.

CHAPTER II

REVIEW OF LITERATURE

The purpose of this interpretive phenomenological study was to examine the individual experiences and perceptions of Baby Boomer industrial security managers and industrial security specialists regarding organizational readiness when Baby Boomers begin to retire. The industrial security employees are located at the United States-based aerospace company with security offices in the Northwest, Southwest, Midwest, and Eastern regions of the country. The industrial security organization is facing Baby Boomer retirements, reduction in work force, terminations, and employment attrition that affect the ability to create or share tacit knowledge among remaining, multi-generational employees.

Organizations face a knowledge and capabilities crisis when Baby Boomers who make up 28% of the workforce are replaced by multi-generational employees (Stevens, 2010). The phenomenological method is a reliable approach that could help organizations with planning and preparing for future population changes in public and private corporations. The Baby Boomer generation industrial security managers and industrial security specialists possess inordinate levels of tacit knowledge valuable to senior leaders in the evaluation of knowledge sharing strategies, processes, and methodologies.

Chapter 2 contains peer-reviewed literature supporting the phenomenological study of knowledge loss occurring when older workers depart organizations. The literature review in Chapter 2 is a logical argument using current research to support the research questions (Shank, 2006). A written summary of journal articles, books, and other references that document the need for the study make up the references contained in this research study.

The goal of the phenomenological study was to examine the impending knowledge loss when older workers depart and organizational readiness to share knowledge. The researcher used the literature review to document the study topic, and revealed how the findings will add to existing literature (Shank, 2006). In qualitative research, it is important the research has not already been done (Shank, 2006). The Chapter 2 literature review documents the understanding of knowledge sharing in an industrial security organization. The literature review examined the research conducted in an effort to add to existing knowledge. The literature review provided a discussion of potential knowledge loss when older workers depart the organization. The research examined organizational readiness to share knowledge among industrial security personnel. The following literature review explored the following resources and methods: title searches, database searches, articles, books, peer reviewed journals, and dissertations. A chapter concluding an analysis of the literature review will be included in the research study. Finally, key points emerged as the study transitions to Chapter 3.

Theories and Concepts.

This section included the philosophy of knowledge, demographics, aging workforce, and concluded with a subtopic of Baby Boomer aerospace workers eligible to retire. Early philosophers wanted to determine how to gain and understand knowledge, and determine the reliability of knowledge. Epistemology is the branch of philosophy directed to sources, nature, and limits of knowledge. The two epistemological traditions of Western philosophy are rationalism and empiricism. Western philosophers agreed knowledge was justified true belief, a concept discussed by Plato in his Meno, Phaedo, and Theaeteus (Nonaka & Takeuchi, 1995). However, rationalism argues that true knowledge is a mental process and is not the product of sensory experience. In this view, the existence of a priori knowledge does not require justification by sensory experience (Nonaka & Takeuchi, 1995). In contrast, empiricists believe no a priori knowledge, with one's sense the only source of knowledge. Knowledge exists when the truth and evidence for what is believed are apparent (Moser & vander Nat, 2003). Philosophers who subscribe to this view accept that everything in the world has intrinsically objective existence (Nonaka & Takeuchi, 1995).

Epistemology is a fundamental theme of philosophers, who found it necessary to coordinate the theory of knowledge with developing scientific thought (Becerra-Fernandez, Gonzalez, & Sabherwal, 2004). Humans come into the world with categories of understanding and try to make sense of unprocessed data. Experiences are validated by testing hypotheses toward an integrated body of scientific knowledge. Early philosophers did not embrace the sensory experience of empirical knowledge, choosing to accept the non-empirical basis, where knowledge depends on evidence (Moser & vander Nat, 2003). Some viewpoints would change to accommodate a paradigm shift toward epistemology. Opposition arose from empiricists, represented by Locke, Berkeley, Hume, Reid, and Kant, who denied the existence of innate ideas altogether (Moser & vander Nat, 2003). The questions about the nature, source, and limits of knowledge motivate epistemology. Moser and vander Nat (2003) stated, "Knowledge requires belief, but belief does not require knowledge" (p. 2). However, knowledge and belief are connected to one another, where truth and justification are required.

Plato would add to the epistemology debate through a rationalistic perspective. He developed the theory of idea described as a form observed from the pure mental eye (Nonanka & Takeuchi, 1995). Plato theorized that knowledge is acquired through the process of recollection, and argued that knowledge can only be of unchanging ideas, which were obtained at birth (Moser & vander Nat, 2003). Plato contended that knowledge is achievable through pre-theoretical comprehension, indicating that knowledge is innate, present in our speech and thought (Franklin, 2009). Aristotle supported Plato's views, but would later acquiesce toward an empiricist (a posteriori) position representing the world through sensory experience and conceptualization, by not relying on reason alone. Aristotle argued that idea or form cannot be isolated from a physical object, nor can it exist independent from sensory perception (Nonaka & Takeuchi, 1995). Researchers and philosophers alike would explain the acquisition of knowledge would examine these contrasting views. In contrast, Aristotelian rationalism held that forms could not exist apart from physical objects, but were instantiated in sensory objects (Moser & vander Nat, 2003). The opposing views indicated conflicting viewpoints among early philosophers about the theory of knowledge.

From a modern perspective, comprehensive epistemology encompasses a unified theory of the mind and the way it works, logic and rational thinking, moral and emotional lives, conscious and unconscious knowledge, and experience (Moser & vander Nat, 2003). As a diverse group of people, our epistemological experience is vast because of differences in nationalities, backgrounds, values, norms, and cultures. Through rationalism, modern philosophers discussed the evolvement of knowledge from the existence of distinctive ideas with an acceptance of data and ideas that originate from experience (Moser & vander Nat, 2003). The shift from rationalism to empiricism would be instrumental in the understanding of epistemology. The empiricists believed that all ideas were rooted in experience from the senses, with no a priori knowledge of the world (Moser & vander Nat, 2003).

Traditional epistemology has its roots in Plato, in the distinction between knowledge and true belief. Knowledge and true belief exemplify the tenets of knowledge management. The justification and evidential relation provide a connection between empiricist and rationalist versions, enabling a distinction between knowledge and true belief (Stanford Encyclopedia of Philosophy, 2007). Therefore, having an understanding of how knowledge is acquired will help in defining if knowledge is believable.

Knowledge Management Theory.

The exploration of knowledge consists of studying past and present knowledge for errors, accuracy, or improvement. Epistemologists offer an opinion between rationalist and empiricist theories and if knowledge attainment is a priori or posteriori (Becerra-Fernandez et al., 2004). Philosophers identified pragmatism as the vehicle for reconciling science with religion and morality (Stanford Encyclopedia of Philosophy, 2008). Organizational leaders benefit from epistemic exploration in the analysis of complex problems, challenging conventions, and identifying groundbreaking solutions. Creativity and original thinking in knowledge management is an essential component to preparing for the retirement and demographic shift that will alter the United States workforce. Knowledge management literature related to epistemology from two perspectives: objectivist and practice-based perspectives on knowledge (Hislop, 2009). The objectivist view is the presumption that knowledge is an entity, which could be codified and separated from the people who have and use knowledge (Hislop, 2009). In contrast, the practice-based perspective assumed that knowledge is embedded in, developed through, and inseparable from people's workplace, practices, and context where they occur (Hislop, 2009). However, as Frederick Taylor's scientific management theory evolved to the human relations theory, organizational theorist began to see a paradigm shift from scientific management to the development of managerial social skills (Drucker, 1999). Peter Drucker's groundbreaking research on the importance of knowledge workers would pave the way for organizational learning toward improving productivity (Drucker, 1999).

Knowledge management is becoming a strategic imperative for global organizations.

Organizations without an effective knowledge management system can lose the competitive advantage during difficult economic conditions. Liyanage, Elhag, Ballal, and Li (2009) stated, "Most of all, knowledge management improves decision-making, engenders learning, facilitates collaboration and networking and also encourages and promotes innovation" (p. 122). Knowledge is becoming the most important asset of all organizations. Within organizations knowledge re-use occurs and becomes inserted in documents, routines, processes, practices, procedures, and norms (Aktharsha., 2011). However, firms with a flexible organizational structure that encourage knowledge sharing, and who can manage knowledge effectively and efficiently can create competitive advantage (Emadzade, Mashayekhi, & Abdar, 2012). The emphasis on technical tools and not people can be detrimental to having a robust knowledge management system in place. Like other programs, knowledge management must demonstrate value and business impact to survive and thrive in global organizations (Aaron, 2009). The systematic management of knowledge organizations can distinguish themselves from their competitors leading to a competitive advantage (Durst & Wilhelm, 2011).

Peter Drucker, the father of knowledge management, recognized knowledge as a key resource for military and economic strength. The 2007-2009 economic collapse reemphasized the need to identify, retain, and share knowledge to improve organizational effectiveness and performance. Frederick Taylor, who was responsible for the scientific management theory, was the first person to apply knowledge to work (Drucker, 1999). The requirement in accomplishing knowledge work is to know 'what the task is,' opposed to manual work in knowing 'how the work is to be accomplished' (Drucker, 1999). The most vital resource in organizations is the collective knowledge residing in knowledge worker minds. Traditional emphasis on knowledge management consisted of processes, procedures, intellectual property, best practices, forecast, lessons learned, and solutions to business problems (Becerra-Fernandez et al., 2004). Organizational knowledge management experts are focusing on acquiring tacit knowledge resident in the minds of workers who are eligible to retire.

Leaders tasked with extricating tacit knowledge from knowledge workers, so information is not reworked, results in improved productivity. Leaders face challenges with developing knowledge management systems to extract tacit knowledge from Baby Boomer employees prior to their departure. Knowledge workers are well educated and experienced, retain knowledge that is not available to everyone, generate their own work standards, and make decisions autonomously requiring different approaches, tools and methods than managing non-knowledge workers (Mládková, 2012). The economic conditions occurring within corporations across the country are resulting in organizational downsizings and Baby Boomer retirements requiring leaders to make better and faster decisions. Today's leaders and managers are faced with developing safeguards to protect intellectual property and finding secure means to share knowledge in all industries.

Dalkir (2011) stated, "knowledge management consists of strategies and processes designed to identify, capture, structure, value, leverage, and share an organization's intellectual asset to enhance its performance and competitiveness" (p. 5).

Organizations are not in a position to react to potential knowledge loss issues if knowledge systems are ineffective. Knowledge management addresses the critical organizational issues of surviving and competitive advantage in response to a changing environment. An organization's intellectual capital is a significant resource for organizations to manage and exploit for its sustainment. Organizations in search of opportunities to reduce cycle time undergo continuous improvement and increased transparency will yield returns if knowledge management processes are a strategic part of the business. Knowledge management describes an organization's conscious strategy of providing the right knowledge to individuals who need it (Calo, 2008).

Before knowledge management occurs, leaders and managers need to understand how knowledge is used. The benefits of successfully managing knowledge are as follows: leveraging core competencies, innovation, improving cycle times, decision making, and strategic benefit. Effective knowledge management requires the implementation of knowledge management processes and procedures. From an organizational perspective, knowledge management aim is to improve organizational performance (Hislop, 2010). Leaders will find it necessary to clarify the knowledge they want to manage before implementing a knowledge management process. The management of knowledge encompasses knowledge creation, sharing, and distribution processes that permeate throughout organizational boundaries.

Effective knowledge management will avoid reinventing processes and procedures and eliminating redundancy. Empirical studies cite the facilitators and inhibitors to knowledge sharing as time required to share knowledge, motivation for sharing, transmission channels, and social structure of the organization (Gupta, Joshi, & Agarwal, 2012). Tacit knowledge is resident in each individual's head requiring leaders to extract, disposition, document, and share it within the organization. The added benefit of a robust knowledge management program is innovation, whether incremental or breakthrough innovations. Effective knowledge management programs focus on knowledge workers who are closest to the organization's operations. However, knowledge workers will be the main focal point in creating, retaining, and using knowledge.

Knowledge workers have portable and valuable capital transferrable to any company making them valuable to the organization strategy. Knowledge workers possessing skills in demand can derail a company if they decide to leave their companies. Leaders and managers face challenges with capturing and preserving tacit knowledge to sustain and grow the organization. Leaders have the responsibility of identifying critical tacit (personal) knowledge to retain, share, and store. Explicit knowledge is words and numbers and shared formally within an organization (DeLong, 2004). This type of knowledge requires codification and distribution to the organization. In contrast, tacit knowledge or non-rational knowledge that is difficult to formalize or share is usually based on experiences or intuitions and activities (Iancu & Buta, 2011). The creation and sharing of tacit knowledge are vital to moving the organization forward to stay competitive and to survive in a shrinking Department of Defense Budget.

Drucker (1999) classified individuals who performed both manual and knowledge work as a technologists. Effective transfer of knowledge requires leaders and managers to have an awareness of organizational processes and strategies of knowledge management systems (Calo, 2008). Organizational leaders who have not taken steps to address the brain drain of Baby Boomer retirements face the possibility of losing a competitive advantage.

The brain drain consists of an exodus of skills, experience, and knowledge that will take time to transfer to remaining employees (Ball & Gotsill, 2011). Mathew and Kavitha (2008) stated, "the transfer of knowledge or code from one member to another helps the organization to earn revenue and gain advantages" (p. 26). The loss of critical knowledge can hurt the competitiveness of most businesses. Organizations focus on sharing non- rational tacit knowledge deriving from experience or intuition of individuals (Iancu & Buta, 2011). Knowledge sharing requires a willingness of individuals to share knowledge by communicating directly or indirectly with some knowledge archive. Further, knowledge sharing represents capturing, organizing, reusing, and transferring experienced-based knowledge in the organization and making that knowledge available to its employees (Ngah & Jusoff, 2009). However, knowledge sharing is voluntary, but it can be encouraged and facilitated by leaders. Leaders are responsible for creating a knowledge sharing culture and behavior within their organizations. The ability of leaders to motivate subordinates during difficult economic times is problematic. Organizational leaders are taking steps to identify and employ knowledge management systems to ensure a competitive advantage.

Trends in Knowledge Management.

The Baby Boomer exodus and lack of qualified employees to take over have spurred organizations to address knowledge management. Organizations are finding innovative opportunities to capture, share, and retain knowledge. The relationship between knowledge management and total quality management enables continuous improvement by using available data within an organization (Honarpour, Jusoh, & Khalil, 2012). The emphasis on managing people versus technology will be essential to sharing knowledge across all domains of an organization. Furthermore, strategic workplace planning is an integral part of retaining knowledge workers, requiring assessment of current and future worker needs to fill employment gaps. Leaders and managers face organizational challenges with employee development strategies that address business goals and objectives. Trugman-Nikol (2011) stated, "The potential loss of knowledge and expertise that could occur when Baby Boomers retire could be catastrophic" (p. 55). As boomers prepare to retire, organizations are concerned with who will replace the departing employees. One approach organizations will employ is to identify knowledge gaps and take appropriate steps to fill the gap through hiring and training. The safeguarding of a company's most valuable asset, employee knowledge, should be a strategic imperative (Trugman-Nikol, 2011). Furthermore, the trend of boomers working beyond retirement will force human resource professionals to identify workforce-planning strategies. Leaders and organizations face knowledge loss if programs not implemented to introduce systems to capture and reuse critical knowledge.

Knowledge Loss.

The economic challenge of the economy is forcing many companies to restructure and produce more with fewer employees (Trugman-Nikol, 2011). Many factors contribute to knowledge loss in corporations, which can hamper creativity and innovation. The following factors contributed to knowledge loss in organizations: not having documented processes and procedures, lacking mentoring and cross training, and standard operating procedure (SOP). Demographic changes are affecting all industries, causing leaders to make knowledge management a strategic priority. The cost of knowledge can take many forms, such as retaining knowledge, reworking, developing knowledge, lost knowledge, and missing knowledge. The Baby Boomer exodus severely affects corporations and industries around the industrialized world. A smaller demographic (multi-generational) is emerging because of low fertility rates, which are replacing the Baby Boomer cohort.

The Baby Boomer generation is highly skilled, educated, and knowledgeable, having long-term positions at one company. The loss of highly skilled employees and the retention of less experienced employees challenge leaders to identity skill gaps and barriers to knowledge capturing and sharing. The reality of lost knowledge is becoming a realization, when employees leave organizations without a plan to share tacit knowledge among remaining employees. As boomers retire, considerable strain rests on the remaining workforce of multi-generational employees. In a recent survey of 140 midsize and large U.S. companies, data indicated that 61% of organizations have or will be developing programs to retain key personnel (Miller, 2009). Ball and Gotsill (2011) emphasized, "The economic meltdown has given leaders and managers a reprieve and an opportunity to craft a knowledge capture and transfer plan that makes sense" (p. 6).

The loss of knowledgeable and experienced boomers in the aerospace arena is problematic because of the technical complexity of the work performed. Peter Senge's systems thinking approach is necessary to solve organizational problems

requiring participation from every product team.
Leaders face challenges with creating learning
organizations that focus on systems thinking.
Organizational leaders are creating learning
environments to exploit individual competence in new
and innovative ways (Aktharsha', 2011). As Singh
(2011) stated, "The knowledge leaders need to
explain the goals of knowledge management so that
people can identify their roles in achieving those
goals" (p. 356). Organizational leaders faced with an
investment and implementation of knowledge
management systems to capture, retain, and share
knowledge if they intend to stay competitive.
Drucker's emphasis on knowledge worker roles as
assets rather than cost accentuates the importance to
organizations. Leaders who can understand and
distinguish between codified and personal knowledge
provide organizations with knowledge sharing
capabilities.

Tacit and Explicit Knowledge.

Michael Polanyi, distinguished scientist turned
philosopher, referred to the rootedness of mental

achievements in the personality of the knowing

person (Blum, 2010). The term tacit knowledge

applies to forms of personal knowledge that is un-

codified, or not in the category of information. Tacit

knowledge cannot be formalized and put into words

and has a presence in the world, which is central to

the knowledge of the world (Polanyi, 1966). In

contrast, Polanyi debated Meno's paradox as

discussed by Plato. Polanyi argued if tacit knowledge

is a central part of knowledge one can know what to

look for and have an idea of what else one wants to

know (Polanyi, 1962). Polanyi distinguished between

tacit and explicit knowledge by stating that one cannot

exist without the other. According to researchers, tacit

knowledge is unique to that individual, situational, and

hard to formalize and disseminate (Nonaka &

Takeuchi, 1995). Explicit knowledge is codified and is

transmitted formally and systematically (Nonaka &

Takeuchi, 1995). The formalization of all knowledge

is essential, because excluding tacit knowledge is

self-defeating. Nonaka and Takeuchi (1995)

emphasized informal knowledge helps to enhance an

organization's learning capability (Siu Loon, 2006).

The transfer, sharing, and retention of tacit knowledge

is paramount to an organization's strategy. The ability to create sustainable knowledge is critical to organizational strategy. Nonaka and Takeuchi, pioneers in the knowledge management field studied innovation and creativity among successful Japanese companies (Dalkir, 2011). In this model, tacit knowledge drives creativity and innovation through self- involvement and commitment necessary in the creation of knowledge (Dalkir, 2011). This model blends Japanese and Western schools of thought in the creation of knowledge.

Knowledge Creating Process.

Knowledge creation and utilization are critical components of a robust knowledge management system. Creating knowledge is vital to an organization's existence, because of the global implications. However, a distinction between knowledge and information is needed, where information is a component necessary for yielding knowledge (Nonaka & Takeuchi, 1995). Leaders and managers decide what knowledge to retain, transfer, or discard as they implement knowledge management systems. Organizational leaders are responsible for developing knowledge management systems, and understanding and communicating the differences between knowledge and information. Their ability to create and use knowledge is critical to an organization sustaining a competitive advantage.

Organizations create and define problems, applying knowledge to solve problems, which leads to the creation of new knowledge through problem solving. Berliant and Fujita (2009) stated, "New knowledge can be produced either individually or jointly, and ideas can be shared with others" (p. 158). The industrial security organization is in a position to benefit from employing knowledge creating strategies to capture knowledge from departing Baby Boomer generation employees using this methodology. The identification of barriers and a reluctance to share knowledge is instrumental to implementing robust knowledge management programs. Leaders and managers tasked with designing knowledge management systems face difficulty with transferring knowledge across organizational boundaries to ensure personnel are equipped with applicable knowledge, information, and data necessary to maintain a competitive advantage. Nonaka and Takeuchi (as cited in Dalkir, 2011) identified four modes towards converting tacit knowledge from explicit knowledge: Socialization, Externalization, Combination, and Internalization (SECI).

Nonaka & Takeuchi's (as cited in Dalkir, 2011) knowledge conversion model consisted of the following: The conversion of tacit knowledge to tacit knowledge is described as socialization; the method of converting tacit to explicit knowledge is called externalization; and the method of converting explicit knowledge to explicit knowledge is described as combination; and the method of converting explicit knowledge to tacit knowledge is called internalization. (p. 66).

Nonaka and Takeuchi's knowledge spiral is a sequential method of knowledge creation necessary toward knowledge flow, sharing, and conversion (as cited in Dalkir, 2011). This model is relevant and applicable to creating and sharing knowledge throughout the organization. The creation of knowledge is continuous and necessary to creating new organizational knowledge, which is essential toward maintaining a competitive advantage (Nonaka

& Takeuchi, 1995). Leaders must acknowledge the importance of tacit knowledge to ensure employees share knowledge across organizational boundaries. From a global perspective, Japanese and Western cultural differences provide an understanding of the obstacles to knowledge sharing in organizations. For example, Western organizations are individual based, explicit knowledge-oriented, with an emphasis on analysis (Nonaka & Takeuchi, 1995). In contrast, Japanese organizations are group based, tacit knowledge- oriented, with an emphasis on experience (Nonaka & Takeuchi, 1995). These inherent differences offer examples of potential obstacles toward motivating employees to share tacit knowledge in any organization.

Knowledge Sharing.

Effective knowledge sharing draws on Peter Blau's social exchange theory where individuals benefit, either monetarily or non-monetarily for sharing knowledge within the organizational improved practices toward the creation of a learning environment for less experienced personnel (Reychav

& Weisberg, 2009). Knowledge sharing is rooted in individual behavior and motivation to share knowledge (Foss, Minbaeva, Pedersen, & Reinholt, 2009). In contrast, the not-invented-here syndrome and employee knowledge hoarding can impede knowledge sharing activities in organizations. Individuals place a higher value on tacit knowledge than explicit knowledge because the former is difficult to replicate (Reychav & Weisberg, 2009). Organizational leaders who can manage sharing tacit related people-specific knowledge lead to a competitive advantage. Scholars have noted intrinsic motivation can enhance knowledge sharing (Foss, Minbaeva, Pedersen, & Reinholt, 2009). Reward and recognition campaigns can be effective inducements to obtaining buy-in to participating in knowledge sharing.

The rewards and recognition program available to managers at the United States- based aerospace company in this study are instrumental in motivating employees to participate and contribute to Process Actions Teams (PAT) and Employee Involvement (EI) initiatives to improve, create, and share knowledge and processes within the industrial security organization. Knowledge sharing leads to organizational efficiencies if employees are actively engaged in exchanging and combining knowledge throughout the organization. Hasan (2011) contended a lack of knowledge sharing contributes to knowledge leaks and results in organizational inefficiency. Organizations face issues with selecting knowledge management practices that encourage sharing (Todorova, 2011). In this study, the United States-based aerospace company relied on subject matter experts assigned on proposal capture teams to exchange knowledge in anticipation of potential contract wins.

Knowledge sharing in the industrial security organization takes into account the contrasting value systems between Baby Boomers and multi-generational cohorts. For example, Generation X individuals grew up with computers, where as Baby Boomer exposure to computers occurred during adulthood. In a recent study, Leiter, Jackson, and Shaughnessy (2009) stated multi-generational employees are more inclined to have job burnout and not participate in knowledge sharing. Therefore, employee retention efforts should be explored in future research studies. People are an organization's most valuable asset, requiring management of people to be at the forefront of organizational strategy, if knowledge sharing is to be successful. The need to have a range of performance management and reward measures motivating employees to share knowledge across all domains is a necessary component of knowledge management. The nurturing of employee professional skills is a key component in motivating employees to create and share knowledge. Once knowledge sharing occurs, leaders will address knowledge retention strategies to decipher the value of knowledge to the organization as a competitive strategy.

A reluctance to share knowledge by industrial security managers and industrial security specialists creates a knowledge hoarding mentality to protect employment (status and stability). Another complication and impediment to knowledge sharing occurs during an economic downturn where employees facing reduction in force refuse to share knowledge with less experienced employees. The failure to share knowledge can assist leaders and managers with employing strategies to effectively capture and retain knowledge. Organizations benefit from knowledge sharing through a positive correlation of receiving non-monetary rewards, improved performance, and employee retention (Reychav & Weisberg, 2009).

An employee's knowledge is critical to defining an organization's effectiveness and competitiveness. Knowledge sharing leads to significant business advantages when leaders tap into the knowledge worker expertise (Reychav & Weisberg, 2009). Knowledge sharing enables an organization better to serve its customers, which can lead to a competitive advantage in the process. Peter Blau's exchange theory explains how a positive exchange process motivates individuals to share willingly with others (Reychav & Weisberg, 2009). Knowledge management theories explain interaction between employees and their organization in the retention of knowledge. Organizations that understand the implications of lost knowledge will invest in knowledge management strategies to capture, retain, share, use, and store knowledge essential to its competitive advantage. Leaders face challenges with observing and reacting to the organizational trends and strategy toward the preservation of knowledge. Critical labor shortages could hamper an organization's ability to create knowledge. Peter Senge's learning organization paradigm change is central to knowledge creation, transfer, and innovation (Senge, 1990).

Knowledge Transfer.

Leaders and managers are beginning to understand the implications of not having a robust knowledge management strategy. A distinction between knowledge reuse, which involves knowledge generated and used by an individual or group, and knowledge creation, where information and data produce new knowledge is necessary for understanding (Watson & Hewett, 2006). An organization's objective is the ability to generate and distribute knowledge to support business strategy, goals and objectives, and competitive advantage. The effective integration of knowledge can lead to an organization acquiring unique capabilities essential to long-term competitive advantage (Ajith Kumar, & Ganesh, 2009). In contrast, the transfer of knowledge occurs through codification and storage into database

repositories accessed and used by individuals
(Watson & Hewett, 2006). Furthermore,
organizational predictors of knowledge transfer are
embedded in employee willingness to transfer
knowledge to each other.

Mathew and Kavitha (2008) examined the
knowledge development stages/cycles to transform
information into knowledge and understanding, and
identified the following. The knowledge development
cycle included: data analysis, knowledge
identification, knowledge creation, and (d) knowledge
development stages. Knowledge development stages
incorporated: (a) knowledge mining and filtering, (b)
knowledge capturing, (c) knowledge storage and
access, (d) knowledge storing and dissemination, (e)
knowledge review, (f) transfer and addition, and (g)
knowledge feedback and change agents (p. 28).

Organizations face knowledge and capabilities
crises when Generation X and Y employees take over
for departing Baby Boomer employees. This research
examined the existing knowledge transfer, retention,
and sharing strategies in an industrial security
organization. Leaders face the challenge of managing
employee retirements and reductions in workforce

that affected the ability to transfer or retain tacit knowledge. The cost and labor associated with knowledge management can be daunting for fledging companies tasked with protecting intellectual property. To stay competitive in any industry requires a shift toward knowledge-based resources. Knowledge is a strategic and important resource in most organizations.

As firms continue to lose employees through attrition, retirements, and layoffs, leaders will look for opportunities to improve the rate of capturing and storing knowledge and ways information is accessed and reused. Knowledge transfer systems are essential components of knowledge management. Leaders must address trust and cultural issues that could affect organizational knowledge transfer opportunities (Gururajan & Fink, 2010). This qualitative study contributed to the knowledge management literature in providing the industrial security leaders with strategies to implement stopgap measures to capture and share knowledge.

The industrial security organization leaders and managers face challenges with employing knowledge management techniques in a unique environment.

The industrial security organization was comprised of three industrial security disciplines: the Department of Defense, Secret Compartmentalized Programs, and Special Program Industrial Security, each having their own knowledge transfer and retention challenges. The decentralization of the production of knowledge offers constraints to knowledge transfer among industrial security personnel (Witt & Zellner, 2009). Contractual requirements provided additional constraints on whom owns the knowledge – the government or contractor. As leaders, the effective management of knowledge will be vital to increasing productivity and staying competitive in the global market. Organizations are valued for their intellectual capital, which overshadows financial capital. For example, General Motors purchased Hughes Aircraft Company (now the United States-based aerospace company) in 1985 to improve dashboard technology on their vehicles. The purchase allowed GM to acquire engineering knowledge it did not possess. Working in a dynamic and fast-paced technological environment has posed interesting challenges. Timely decisions are required, but managers cannot make these decisions without effective knowledge management systems in place. Corporate downsizing during the late 1980s and early 1990s contributed to lost knowledge, with the loss of highly technical and skilled positions. Communication between managers and employees is a critical aspect of knowledge transfer, which highlights the importance of member-to-member interaction. The ability to motivate employees to transfer knowledge is a critical aspect to moving knowledge forward.

The recent economic downturn (2008 – 2014) has resulted in thousands of laid off employees from all job sectors. Managers and leaders are responsible for identifying the skills and resources needed to meet critical program and organization milestones. The tools and techniques used to implement knowledge sharing in any organization should be in place before implementation of a knowledge management system. The use of both tacit and explicit knowledge is dependent on acquiring knowledge from two levels. Organizationally, knowledge dissemination occurs through expertise and experiences based on core competencies, and external sources, such as customers, suppliers, and partners (Aerospace Industries Association, 2010). Managers are responsible for creating a knowledge management system that fosters knowledge transfer and sharing among skilled workers. The organizational dilemma is to determine what knowledge to retain or discard, and what knowledge is of value to the organization.

Organizational knowledge transfer strategy in the industrial security arena will focus on the high demand of tacit knowledge of how to perform a particular task. Trust can lead to mutual problem solving, facilitating knowledge transfer, by creating a sense of security (Jiun-Shiu Chen & Lovvorn, 2011). An understanding of an aerospace company's organizational structure would help one understand the generation of tacit knowledge. The industrial security organization supported all Department of Defense (DoD) programs and special access programs activities within the aerospace enterprise. The industrial security organization relied on external relationships with the following: DoD, business partners, customers, and benchmarking with competitors to improve efficiencies. Internal interaction takes place between legal, human resources, facilities, ethics, supplier management, Information Technology, and communications. Senior industrial security leaders continued to professionalize the organization by requiring college degrees for staff members in the creation of Process Action Teams (PAT), continuting training and education, leadership development, and executive mentoring opportunities. As a benchmarking exercise, the industrial security organization continues to lead similar sized aerospace competitors through innovation, creativity, and process improvements in response to a reduced Department of Defense budget. An organizational leader's ability to transfer usable knowledge rests with the identification of obstacles to effective knowledge transfer.

Barriers to Knowledge Transfer.

Knowledge is a critical organizational asset requiring a strategy for capturing, retaining, sharing, and storing it for use among employees. The Bureau of Labor Statistics (BLS) identified the following industries suffering from the boomer exodus: manufacturing, educational services, public administration, and health services (Ball & Gotsill, 2011). However, proactive organizations have identified potential knowledge transfer problems prior to knowledge transfer. Knowledge transfer barriers occur because of not understanding what knowledge is and not really comprehending how to get started (Ball & Gotsill, 2011). Global implications add another obstacle to effective knowledge management, as companies comply with local and state laws. Other obstacles include conflicting goals inside and between organizations, lack of incentives, and the absence of knowledge curriculum (Ball & Gotsill, 2011). Furthermore, incompatible systems and processes can inhibit knowledge transfer internally or externally within the organization. According to organizational theorists, knowledge management practices are disjointed, expensive, and time consuming and unable to keep up with changing economic conditions (McLaughlin & Stankosky, 2010). Leaders possessing an open mind toward knowledge transfer are an essential component to creating a culture of knowledge transfer. The identification of knowledge transfer impediments will lead to a smooth transition during the knowledge transfer process. Organizational leaders must be intimately involved with the process of identifying usable and non-usable knowledge before implementation of knowledge management systems. Organizational leaders do face challenges with creating a knowledge-sharing environment to stimulate employees to become involved in knowledge sharing activities.

Knowledge Retention Processes and Strategies.

Organizational tacit knowledge retention strategies involve the recruiting of subject matter experts to share knowledge with less experienced employees. The ability to recruit and retain highly skilled employees can increase an organization's competitive advantage. Organizational human resource leaders faced challenges of creating work and employment arrangements conducive to older workers. A cultural change is to debunk the myths that older workers are not creative or innovative. Employers will contend with ageism and age related stereotypes that could result in task conflict, emotional conflict, and behavioral disintegration (Stark, 2009). For example, the United States-based aerospace company recently turned to retired program managers and executives to help with certifying their new commercial aircraft, which consisted of the fuselage, composed of composite materials. A corporate culture change is necessary to embrace older workers who desire to stay and work into their retirement.

Creating a collaborative work environment will be conducive to knowledge retention in organizations committed to their people. The creation of a phased retirement program for retirement-aged employees who want to continue working is necessary to retain top talent. The creation of a retiree network will keep knowledge flowing back into the organization, when employees are retired. The implementation of flexible work hours for retirement-aged employees is an incentive to keep them employed. Continuous training and education help employees deepen their knowledge and skills. A job sharing opportunity of matching older workers with younger workers ensures the transfer of tacit knowledge. Oftentimes, an employee is not ready to retire, especially if he or she is a valued contributor to the success of the company. As an example, the United States-based aerospace company created a research and technology organization to identify advanced technologies to ensure competitive growth and sustainment.

Mentorship programs provide older workers with opportunities to give back to the company and to ensure knowledge transfers on to younger less experienced employees. However, the identification and tracking of knowledge management trends can help managers position the organization toward improved competitive advantage. More important, leaders who can transform organizations will be critical to moving organizations forward to capture, share, and reuse knowledge.

Transformational and Transactional Leadership.

The ability of leaders to motivate employees is essential to establishing organizational knowledge management systems encompassing effective knowledge sharing. Effective leadership is essential toward motivating employees to create and share knowledge in a global economy, where failure could lead to loss of competitive advantage and market share. James McGregor Burns (1978) was responsible for influencing transformational leadership (as cited in Yukl, 2010). Theoretical implications for knowledge sharing are exhibited by subordinates showing trust, admiration, and loyalty toward the leader; thus, motivating them to do more than expected (Yukl, 2010). A key component in follower motivation is to share knowledge in a global economy. Transformational leaders request that followers forego their self-interest for the benefit of the group, organization, and society (Bass, 1990).

However, Bass (1990) posited transformational leadership supplements transactional leadership as a systemic process to bring about change. Transactional leaders obtain follower compliance through an exchange process, void of enthusiasm to completion of their tasks (Yukl, 2010). Leadership theorist suggests a blending of transformational and transactional leadership toward organizational effectiveness. Tansformational leadership relies on follower motivation to perform while transactional leaders emphasize an exchange toward task completion (Yukl, 2010). Effective leaders adopt a combination of transformational and transactional leadership qualities, which can be useful to motivating followers to understand organizational benefits of sharing knowledge across organizational boundaries. Global organizational leaders must understand and be sensitive to cultural differences. Transformational leaders face challenging diversity issues in the creation of knowledge management systems in response to changing business climates (Paulienė, 2012). Globalization leaders should be cognizant of the cultural differences that could affect knowledge sharing in organizations. While there are various leadership styles, it is imperative to know what global business leaders value leadership skills and knowledge (Paulienė, 2012).

Transformational leaders can move organizations forward in becoming learning organizations where knowledge is shared and leads to innovation. Organizational strategy focusing on continuous learning requires an ongoing investment in transformational leadership skills are needed to support organizational innovation (Soliman, 2011). Transformational leaders, who motivate employees in the knowledge transfer process, are critical to gaining a competitive advantage. Organizations require transformational leaders who can implement effective knowledge management programs as a strategic initiative (Soliman, 2011). Transformational leadership is important to creation of organizational

knowledge using team collaboration and employee
engagement efforts (Hoon, Kolb, Hee, & Kyoung,
2012). Nonaka and Takeuchi's seminal work on
knowledge creation is critical to transformational
leadership development of empowered, engaged, and
dedicated workers. An examination of the leader-
member exchange theory is another opportunity to
motivate followers to share what they know.

Leader-Member Exchange Theory (LMX).

Leadership is an important component toward
influencing organizational knowledge sharing in
industries. George Graen's Leader-Member
Exchange Theory (LMX) is an important construct to
understanding the role of leaders toward influencing
knowledge sharing across organizational boundaries
(Schermerhorn et al., 2003). This dyadic leadership
theory focuses on the quality of the working
relationship between leader and follower
(Schermerhorn, Hunt, & Osborn, 2003). In this
construct, the leader establishes a one-on-one
relationship with each follower, with the relationship
based on trust and expectation displayed by leader

and follower (Nahavandi, 2006). Therefore, leadership theorists suggested a high-quality LMX correlates to an increase in follower satisfaction and productivity while a low-quality LMX correlates to a decrease in follower satisfaction (Schermerhorn et al., 2003). A high-quality leader member exchange results in members having organizational commitment (Hu, Tsung-Lin, Haw-Jeng, & Lee-Cheng, 2012). Organizational leaders with the ability to establish meaningful relationships with followers through trust, respect, and loyalty are essential to fostering an environment of exchanges (Wilson, Sin, & Conlon, 2010).

Nahavandi (2006) posited that LMX theory is central to the leader's ability to establish one-on-one connections with their followers. Leaders will forge diverse relationships with each follower based on the quality of the exchange. Followers with high-quality LMX have a mutual admiration for leaders with the expectation of continued professional growth (Nahavandi, 2006). The LMX theory offers leaders a vehicle toward motivating followers to share knowledge in a competitive and global environment. Successful leaders create environments of trust essential to knowledge sharing and innovation. A correlation exists when knowledge is shared leading to innovations necessary to maintain a competitive advantage (Hu, Tsung-Lin, Haw-Jeng, & Lee-Cheng, 2012). More important, organizations with transformational and leader-member exchange leaders can lead to greater promotion of organizational and relational identification, which can lead to greater knowledge sharing (Carmeli, Atwater, & Levi, 2011). Organizational theorists recognize the value of transferring and sharing knowledge as a vehicle to innovation (Carmeli, Atwater, & Levi, 2011). However, organizations not positioned to create knowledge management systems risk knowledge loss when employees depart the organization. Social exchange theory is an essential component toward effective organizational knowledge sharing.

Social Exchange Theory.

Peter Blau's groundbreaking social exchange theory focuses on individual actions when motivated by expected rewards (Reychav & Weisberg, 2009). Furthermore, the social exchange theory explores collaborative behaviors that might go unrewarded by the organization (Watson & Hewett, 2006). Corporate leaders and managers determine specific knowledge to retain as a competitive advantage. Social exchange theorists posited that innovation is accepted and expected of leaders in dealing with difficult organizational problems (Yukl, 2010).

The theoretical component of knowledge sharing, introduced by Blau's (1964) exchange theory or voluntary action by individuals and the return they bring. Blau examined the social exchange theory, which expressed why individuals are dedicated to the organization. Effective knowledge sharing can lead to improving an organization's competitive advantage. Blau's social exchange theory examined the monetary relationship where the benefits of exchange outweigh the cost (Reychav & Weisberg, 2009). In contrast, a non-monetary social exchange relationship occurs when individuals develop a positive exchange based on trust by each party (Reychav & Weisberg, 2009). Understanding knowledge-sharing behaviors helps managers in creating organizational strategies to encourage individuals to share knowledge in their organizations. This theory examined the understanding of the motivation for sharing knowledge in an industrial security organization. The creation of knowledge through sharing processes can influence organizational performance and competitive advantages. In comparison, knowledge retention efforts are essential aspects to an organization's strategic direction. However, organizational knowledge management systems are essential to sustaining a competitive advantage.

Learning Organizations.

Peter Senge's, Fifth Discipline, outlines the following steps organizations must take to create a learning organization: (a) adopt systems thinking, (b) encourage personal master, (c) bring mental models to the forefront and challenge them, (d) build a shared vision, and (e) emphasize shared learning (Nonaka & Takeuchi, 1995). The highly complex nature of organizations provides justification for Senge's (1990) system of thinking in the integration of reason and intuition. Senge (1990), a pioneer in systems thinking, described thinking as a conceptual framework, with knowledge and tools to help one imagine how to modify the changes effectively. Organizational changing demographics challenge leaders and managers to create knowledge management systems to accommodate Baby Boomer retirements, reduction in force, and terminations. Organizational learning is critical to the long-term success and strategy by learning faster than the competition (Stancu & Balu, 2009).

A learning organization is critical to employee development by linking individual performance with organizational performance, and sharing knowledge among individuals (Stancu & Balu, 2009). Effective learning requires individuals to think, communicate, and cooperate, which increases an individuals' ability to learn (Stancu & Balu, 2009). Organizational complexity is increasing causing leaders to rely on a systems thinking approach to solve difficult problems. According to Senge, systems and learning contributed to the learning organization as a theory of personal change and organizational transformation (as cited in Caldwell, 2012). Organizations require a systems-thinking approach because of the complexities required to compete in a global environment (Senge, 1990). Organizations employing a systems-thinking approach require a leader who can lead change and engage everyone (Caldwell, 2012). Furthermore, communities of practice (CoP) can assist organizational leaders with an expansion of knowledge among individuals.

Communities of Practice.

Organizations that do not innovate can lose their competitive advantage in the global economy. Effective knowledge management is a vehicle to bridging the organizational gap toward improving productivity and efficiencies. Knowledge management is an increasingly important component that includes databases, documents, policies and procedures, and the tacit knowledge resident in the minds of employees (Krishnaveni & Sujatha, 2012). Global organizations forced to innovate and create opportunities to improve competitive advantage can be at a disadvantage when competing with innovative and creative companies. A community of practice (CoP) occurs when a group of individuals with similar concerns about a problem expands their knowledge through group interaction (Krishnaveni & Sujatha,

2012). Organizations must be poised to retain, develop, organize, and use employee knowledge and experience (Haller-Hayon, 2011). Organizations are experiencing knowledge loss from departing employees before the implementation of knowledge sharing initiatives. The creation of learning organizations can close the gap by adopting a multi-dimensional learning model (Haller-Hayon, 2011). Organizations are becoming learning organizations, where the community rather than the individual is the learner (Haller- Hayon, 2011).

This is an alternate approach to individual knowledge sharing activities wherein employees become unmotivated to share knowledge, for fear of layoffs, or hoarding knowledge. Learning organizations are critical to improving workforce development through action learning (LaRue, Childs, & Larson, 2004). Action learning is similar to communities of practice, where both try to work around traditional organizational structures and barriers to change (LaRue et al., 2004). Action learning teams consists of critical stakeholders tasked with developing new capabilities and identifying process gaps and behavioral barriers (LaRue et al.,

2004). The relationship between knowledge management and communities of practice toward transferring knowledge is important to the development of effective knowledge management systems (Krishnaveni & Sujatha, 2012).

Individuals who participate in a CoP are individuals who have commonalities gained from effective teaming and collaboration (Krishnaveni & Sujatha, 2012). In this scenario, the CoP is informal allowing people to communicate and interact in an open environment of trust crossing organizational boundaries. Fostering of organizational trust can increase the use of personalization and codification strategy (Windsperger & Gorovaia, 2010). Further, Blau's (1964/2008) social exchange theory promotes trust and respect as a mechanism for voluntary actions motivated by the returns employees are expected to receive. The practice of interpersonal relationships is stressed where learning can occur through vigorous participation in the situation (Lawthom, 2011). The challenges of sharing knowledge with reluctant employees could be costly to organizations. Therefore, employee empowerment is instrumental to an effective CoP, where leaders do

not force teamwork when the situation does not
dictate it (Kirkman, Mathieu, Cordery, Rosen, &
Kukenberger, 2011). An effective CoP can provide a
competitive advantage when leaders actively manage
and support a collaborative process. However, labor
shortages could impede an organization's effort to
create effective knowledge management systems if
the talent walks out the door.

Skilled Labor Shortage.

Organizations are facing a loss of critical tacit
knowledge because of Baby Boomer retirements,
reduction in work force, and attrition. The loss of a
highly skilled workforce is becoming a reality, where
employee retention efforts are becoming a strategic
imperative. Knowledge sharing is an essential
component of any knowledge management system,
especially in the industrial security organization.
Successful knowledge sharing can help organizations
to build on employees' past experience and
knowledge, problem solve, innovate, and avoid
rework (Cyr & Chun, 2010). As a strategy, the United
States-based aerospace company human resources

specialists identified 0-5 year tenure employees as the target population to retain. The recent economic downtown has stymied the conversation about Baby Boomer retirements, but a rebounding economy will reignite retirements. A combination of job dissatisfaction and demographic trends contribute to knowledge retention efforts within organizations. The skilled labor shortage correlates to Baby Boomer retirements and a lack of student interest in math and science. A shortage of knowledge workers will affect organizations beyond the Baby Boomer exodus. The impending exodus of Baby Boomers represents a loss of individuals with high levels of experience and skills (Ball & Gotsill, 2011). The shortage affects two groups: managers and skilled workers in high-tech positions. The economic recession and declining Department of Defense budget reductions have affected the reorganization and restructuring of the aerospace industry.

Leaders and managers are retooling to provide a learning environment that fosters continuous training and education. Organizational leaders must invest in employee retention strategies and opportunities that focus on the zero to 5-year employees. The needs of multi-generational employees are vastly different from the traditional and baby boom generation employees. A strategy is necessary to ensure Baby Boomer tacit knowledge is at the forefront of Chief Executive Officers (CEO) minds.

A critical component of knowledge retention in the aerospace industry consists of individuals who maintain a United States industrial security clearance. This is an added incentive to retain and transfer knowledge within the industrial security organization. Obtaining an industrial security clearance is expensive and time-consuming taking approximately one year or more to attain. The level of security clearance correlates to the sensitivity of the work performed, customer approval, background investigation, and contractual requirement. The loss of an individual with an industrial security clearance beyond the top-secret level can be detrimental to the program and company. For example, if an adequate number of personnel cannot obtain a clearance, a potential contract can be terminated, and be resubmitted as a request for proposal to a competitor. Another effect to knowledge retention in the

aerospace industry is the problem of multi-
generational employees failing to pass a background
investigation because of financial or criminal
disclosures. Furthermore, the industrial security
manager population average age is 46.5, all
possessing bachelor, masters, and doctoral degrees,
with 15 managers eligible to retire in five years or less
if they exercise their retirement eligibility option.

The ability of corporate leaders to recognize
and develop a robust knowledge management
infrastructure further emphasizes progressive
leadership. The focus on capturing tacit knowledge
from retirement-aged employees who retain
undocumented processes and procedures in their
heads is critical to organizational growth and
sustainment. The industrial security organization
focus is on becoming a learning organization, in which
leaders will teach and guide employees to shape their
futures. As Dalkir (2011) posited, "Knowledge has to
be captured and codified in such a way that it can
become a part of the existing knowledge base of the
organization" (p. 99). Long-term experiences in
working in the industrial security arena provide
personnel unique knowledge, especially the silo effect

within the department, because of the sensitive nature of the data and processes.

A knowledge management infrastructure should encompass mentoring opportunities and human resource involvement in revising job roles and responsibilities of individuals who will retire within five years. As cited in Nonaka and Nishiguchi, "With the conversion of tacit knowledge held by individuals into organizational knowledge, knowledge goes up, both in scale and at ontological levels" (Nonaka & Nishiguchi, 2001, p. 27). Leader and employee involvement is instrumental in developing a robust knowledge management infrastructure for the industrial security organization to include strategic alignment with business operational goals and objectives.

Worker Demographics.

In the next 10 years, the labor force will experience an increase in Baby Boomers, who will be between 50-68 years of age in 2014 (Toossi, 2005). Organizations with traditional workers make up a small cohort of people born between 1922 and 1944.

Traditional worker values shaped by key historical events with an emphasis on conformity, honor, and discipline (Durkin, 2010). Between 1946 and 1964, the fertility rate increased by 25% of the U.S. population to 76 million people (Toossi, 2009). This segment of the population is pivotal to understanding the problem of lost knowledge, when Baby Boomer employees leave the workplace. Between 1965 and 1975, a decline in the number of births occurred which led to a smaller population denoted as baby bust or Generation X individuals who will be between 25 to 54 years of age from 2004 to 2014 (Toossi, 2005).

Finally, baby boom echo, referred to as Generation Y or Nexters, are comprised of children of baby boom generation parents after 1980 and until 1995, who grew up in the Information Age (Toossi, 2005). The Generation X group will be a viable workforce by 2014 (Toossi, 2009). Decreased Generation X populations work life balance would need to increase to offset decreased labor balance (Toossi, 2005). The effect will be significant in all industries if knowledge management systems are not implemented to thwart the baby boom exodus.

Demographic trends over the next six years reveal a 60% decrease in the labor pool by 2016 (Stevens, 2010).

By 2018, almost all of the boomers will be 55 years and older. The Baby Boomer demographic changes will adversely affect organizations that do not have robust knowledge management systems in place to transfer and share tacit knowledge. Increased life expectancy and decreased fertility rates are contributors to an aging population and labor force (Toossi, 2005). The implications range beyond the loss of knowledge. For example, technology booms in China and India led to foreigners returning home to work in knowledge industries (Wadhwa, 2009). This change is significant in the ability of the United States to sustain a competitive technical advantage and keep pace with the global community. Adverse effects occur from the reduction of H-1B visas limiting the research fields and information access of non-US scientists (No & Walsh, 2010). The aging workforce and knowledge loss pose significant problems for United States corporations if knowledge-sharing initiatives are not implemented to capture and share existing knowledge.

Aging Workforce.

The US labor force is aging and becoming more diverse, and consisting of more females (Toossi, 2012). The increased growth rate among older workers prompts organizations to adopt strategies to capture and share knowledge. Older aerospace workers possess tacit knowledge cultivated over years of experience performing complex tasks. Kooij, de Lange, Jansen, and Dikkers (2008) stated, "As mentioned, the term 'older worker' may refer to workers from the age of 40 to those aged over 75" (p. 365). According to Toossi (2012) "The annual growth rate of the U.S. labor force over the 2010-2020 period is projected to be 0.7 percent, lower than the 0.8-percent growth rate exhibited in the previous decade" (p. 43). In 2020 Baby Boomers will be between 56 and 74 years old, putting them in the 55-year and older age group (Toossi, 2012). The inherent difference is that Baby Boomer aged employees are working longer because of the financial difficulties caused by lost jobs and the depressed housing market and economic collapse occurring between the years 2007 and 2009. The passage of boomers into higher age groups will lead to an increase in the median age to 41.6 in 2016.

The economic collapse of 2007-2009 (Ball & Gotsill, 2011) is forcing older workers to forgo retirement and work longer, resulting in the commingling of the four worker cohorts. Leaders and managers face challenges with integrating four generations at the same time and acquiescing to flexible work arrangements for older workers. In 2020, Baby Boomers will be older than 55 years of age with retirement on the horizon (Toossi, 2012). The United States is not alone in the demographic shift. In Europe, Boomers are set to exit the workforce in large numbers. From an organizational perspective, Baby Boomer retirements can cause a brain drain that could jeopardize a competitive advantage in knowledge intensive firms.

Aerospace Workers and Retirement.

Corporations are acutely aware of worker departures through retirements, attrition, and the economic recession that has plagued the United

States and abroad. The industry-wide problem of not capturing tacit knowledge from departing employees is detrimental to a company's growth, productivity, and competitive advantage. The Aerospace Industries Association (AIA) identified the loss of intellectual capital caused by a retiring workforce as a critical issue for the success of the industry (Aerospace Industries Association, 2010). If America's aerospace workforce is to survive, corporations must address the following issues, Generation X employees switching jobs, alternate work strategies, virtual workspace is preventing mentoring, loss of critical skills, alternate sourcing strategies, immigration laws, loss of manpower because of outsourcing, and the culture of knowledge hoarding (Aerospace Industries Association, 2010).

A two-fold problem exists with impending retirements and a lack of qualified replacements at all employment levels. During the 1990s, a reduction in Department of Defense funding contributed to a decrease of aerospace companies from 50 major defense contractors down to five. The Aerospace Commission contended the employment shortfall has yet to be recuperated, which contributes to the Baby

Boomer generation knowledge loss.

Corporations should engage in workforce planning to ensure skill gaps receive attention as a result of the Baby Boomer exodus. The Baby Boomer exodus is responsible for the critical shortage of younger workers in all industries, who may not have the necessary skills or experience to backfill the organization (Dychtwald & Baxter, 2007). New challenges emerge for organizational leaders to design corporate strategies that address older workers who want to continue working beyond retirement age. Organizational development practitioners must collaborate with human resource professionals in the design of organization intervention opportunities. The identification of industrial security skills gap is necessary to stay ahead of competitors and drive innovation and creativity.

Multi-Generational Workplace Aerospace Workers and Retirement

A two-fold problem exists with impending retirements and a lack of qualified replacements at all employment levels. During the 1990s, a reduction in Department of Defense funding contributed to a decrease of aerospace companies from 50 major defense contractors down to five. The Aerospace Commission contended the employment shortfall has yet to be recuperated, which contributes to the Baby Boomer generation knowledge loss.

Four generations are coexisting at once in most organizations: Traditionalist (born 1922 to 1945), Baby Boomers (born 1946-1964), Generation X (born 1965-1979), and, Echo Boomers, or Gen-Net (born 1980 to 1995) and the largest cohort since the Baby Boomers (Meisel & Fearon, 2007). Organizational differences can be problematic because of the inherent management challenges. For example, traditional cohorts follow the chain of command, Baby Boomers follow their own method, Generation X individuals work to change command, and Generation Y collaborate (Meisel & Fearon, 2007). This organizational phenomenon may not change because of Baby Boomer departures. Organizations must work with individuals who are empowered and free from hierarchy. Generation Y individuals are growing up in a global environment relying on a virtual workspace without face-to-face interaction with a manager or their teammates. Leaders face a daunting challenge of managing four generations toward diverse thoughts and efficiencies, to avoid misunderstandings and improve productivity. Leaders will have knowledge of each generation if they are to co-exist. For example, young workers want flexible schedules, and tend to be mobile and willing to experiment. Mid-career workers want time for family and community and refuse to miss key events in the lives of their children. Mature workers react to command and control authority, while Baby Boomers prefer a highly structured learning environment, Generation X wants more flexibility in the workplace, and Generation Y are technology proficient (Ball & Gotsill, 2011).

Motivating factors for Generation X employees are vastly different from factors for Baby Boomers. Organizational loyalty and the psychological contracts of employment for life are not appealing to Generation X employees. The impending layoffs across all industries encourage Generation X employees to exhibit detachment from their employer. Corporations are promoting diversity in their organization through hiring to support global activities, which challenges leaders to enhance training toward a multi-generational and diverse workforce. The ability to interact with individuals from different cultures enhances a leader's ability to capture knowledge that could be lost when employees depart from the organization. Advancements in technology in scientific domains have led to an increase of knowledge-intensive work. However, knowledge loss of departing employees and management emphasis on operational activities could affect knowledge retention efforts. Organizations mandated to create meaningful knowledge management processes to improve organizational learning do not have the luxury of waiting. Furthermore, there is a lack of attention to factors that motivate employee knowledge-sharing behaviors occurring in the organization (Blau, 1964).

Skills Gap in Aerospace Industry.

A skills gap occurs when current capabilities and the skills are deficient, requiring leaders and managers to identify stopgap measures. As boomers retire in greater numbers organizations face challenges of a potential loss of highly skilled knowledge workers (Dychtwald & Baxter, 2007). The survey of 150 senior executives, conducted by Robert Half International, rated the trends that would alter the workforce over the next decade, with 47% indicating Baby Boomer retirements as the number one trend (Ball & Gotsill, 2011). Organizations are observing the following: older workers working into their retirement years, realizing the value of mature workers, laws and policies adjusted to accommodate mature workers, and best practices developed to recruit, engage, motivate, and retain mature workers (Dychtwald & Baxter, 2007). The knowledge embodied in individuals accumulated through years of experience and is the hardest to manage and transfer.

Organizations cease to grow or be competitive when a gap in skills occurs, which can permeate beyond industry. Organizational leaders challenged with filling skill gaps they ignored during the recession (Galagan, 2010). The transition to a knowledge society contributed to the hiring of knowledge workers, who perform tasks involving information, products, or services, which comprises the bulk of work performed in the United States. The Baby Boomer generation has a high degree of experience, education, and experience, making it difficult to fill those gaps. The advent of knowledge work led to an emphasis on an educated and knowledgeable workforce. In knowledge work, the task does not program the worker; workers have autonomy and responsibility (Drucker, 1999). The loss of tacit knowledge is problematic, unless corporations embrace a robust knowledge management strategy from top-down and bottom-up to create, retain, and share knowledge. Leaders and managers tasked with managing a multi-generational workforce, with mature workers electing to work past retirement. A shortage of high tech professionals threatens the innovation potential of the United States if foreign-born inventors, who make up 30% of the non-US-born population, cannot enter the United States in the future (No & Walsh, 2010). The coming knowledge and capability shortage requires attention by corporate leaders and become part of their everyday standard operating procedure and corporate strategy. Organizational acknowledgement and inclusion of a multi-generational workforce is an opportunity toward creating, retaining, and sharing knowledge.

Gaps in Literature.

The shift from utilizing product-based resources, processes, and technologies as a competitive market strategy to human capital is occurring in knowledge sharing organizations (Reychav & Weisberg, 2009). However, leaders and managers face the challenge of encouraging and assisting their employees with knowledge sharing. This literature was limited to one aerospace corporation, which hampers the reliability of the phenomenological study. An expansion of the study to include public and private sector industries yielded the opportunity to move knowledge forward to learn if knowledge management systems are in place to sustain a competitive advantage. Furthermore, the study focused on an industrial security organization opposed to the larger engineering population. The exploration of knowledge sharing opportunities and challenges in a United States-based aerospace company included the commercial aircraft organization as another gap that requires examination in future research. A focus on the service organization opposed to the manufacturing organization could add to the gap in the literature. Finally, a lack of empirical research of male and female managers who fail to transfer knowledge to multi-generational employees contributed to a gap in the literature.

Conclusions

The demographic shift of Baby Boomer generation individuals and a lack of experienced multi-generational employees to fill the gap are problematic for organizational leaders (Daud & Yusoff, 2010). This research study provided an analysis of the application and execution of a broad-based knowledge management system. Furthermore, emphasis on the management of people takes on management responsibility and engagement with their employees. This study was instrumental to identifying knowledge management systems required to keep organizations ahead of their competition. A shift from resources, work processes, and technology to a focus on human capital is a paradigm shift organizations should adhere to (Reychav & Weisberg, 2009). Effective knowledge management systems assist with knowledge transfer and sharing. The sharing of knowledge among employees yields knowledge creation and use within an aerospace industrial security organization. More important, leadership will play a key role in moving the corporations toward learning organizations, where competitive advantage improves.

Summary

Chapter 2 provided a historical and philosophical overview of knowledge management. The philosophical aspect of knowledge addressed rationalism and empiricism. Rationalism argues that true knowledge is a mental process and not sensory experience. However, the shift from rationalism to empiricism was instrumental in understanding epistemology. Organizations benefit from epistemic exploration as a method of analyzing complex problems in the workplace. Frederick Taylor's Scientific Management theory (Drucker, 1999) was the catalyst from moving from manual work to knowledge work, leading to a paradigm shift by transforming and integrating management with workers. Peter Drucker (1999) agreed with Frederick

Taylor's theory that manual work consisted of simple, repetitive motions. Corporations faced with the challenge of identifying applicable knowledge used to stay competitive. Knowledge management is a strategic initiative using technology, processes, practices, and cultural change toward sharing knowledge in organizations (Anantatmula, 2009).

Demographic employment shift data provided insight into the coming knowledge shortage when boomers begin to leave organizations through attrition, layoff, and retirement. Baby Boomer industrial security managers may not have a strategy in place to capture tacit knowledge, nor transferring it to multi-generational industrial security non-managers. The United States-based aerospace company Baby Boomer exodus could leave a void in science, engineering, and manufacturing arenas that could jeopardize award of future government contracts. The skills gap of lost tacit knowledge adversely affects organizational productivity and effectiveness. Leaders and mangers face challenges with identifying retention strategies to offset lost knowledge and loss of competitive advantage.

In the literature review the researcher

examined the analysis of knowledge management in organizations, to include the urgency to implement a strategy for capturing tacit knowledge. Transformational, transactional, and leader-member exchange theories were introduced as a vehicle to implementing effective learning and communities of practice models. Peter Blau's social exchange theory was instrumental to understanding why subordinates become obligated to their supervisors beyond their formal employee contract (Settoon, Bennett, & Liden, 1996). The importance of knowledge transfer in an industrial security organization of a major aerospace company was the impetus for this research. Industrial security leaders and managers face challenges with identifying knowledge management strategies for knowledge transfer, retention, and sharing methods in an industrial security organization. Chapter 3 examined the phenomenological method and its application toward knowledge loss among Baby Boomer managers and security specialists in an industrial security organization. Chapter 3 provided the foundation for employing a phenomenological methodology and the intent to address the research questions.

CHAPTER III
METHODS AND PROCEDURES

The purpose for conducting this interpretive phenomenological study was to explore the individual experiences and perceptions of aerospace company industrial security managers and industrial security specialists and the potential loss of knowledge and organizational readiness when Baby Boomers retire. The qualitative phenomenological study focus is on the researcher obtaining a concrete description of the phenomenon, transforming each meaning unit into expressions of the phenomenon (Giorgi & Giorgi, 2008). The purpose of a phenomenological study is to evoke emotion from participants rather than to speak in an authoritarian manner (Bloor & Wood, 2006). The study's significance is important to the aerospace company's competitiveness in capturing future classified DoD contracts. Additionally, the study benefited similar aerospace companies in creating and understanding knowledge management systems. The study provided the aerospace company's Security Fire and Protection (SF&P) leaders with realistic observations of employee willingness to share knowledge.

A purposeful sampling frame selection occurred because the study participants have stories to tell about their lived experiences regarding organizational readiness when Baby Boomers begin to retire (Creswell, 2012). The 20 Baby Boomer security professionals represented a sample from a population of 550 industrial security personnel representing the Northwest, Southwest, Midwest, and Eastern regions of the county. The participants are subject matter experts (SME) within the United States-based government security organization. The selection criteria designed to identify senior level security professionals responsible for multi-billion dollar programs within a United States-based aerospace company. In this study the researcher chose to identify Baby Boomer industrial security managers and security specialists who were eligible to retire in 5 to 10 years, located at the United States-based aerospace company security offices in the

Northwest, Southwest, Midwest, and Eastern regions of the country. The interviewees answered six demographic and nine semi-structured, open-ended personal interview questions. The researcher read a script describing the intent of the research study to each research participant to identify roles. Ten industrial security managers and 10 industrial security specialists were interviewed by telephone and face-to-face to solicit knowledge sharing lived experiences within an industrial security organization. The data was analyzed, coded, stored, organized, and reported using the qualitative analysis software QSR ATLAS.ti 7 to develop effective knowledge creation and sharing strategies and procedures within an industrial security organization. The use of ATLAS.ti 7 assisted in organizing and managing sources, themes, analysis, and findings.

Chapter 3 focused on the methodologies for conducting the study to observe and understand the lived experiences and perceptions of industrial security managers and industrial security specialists regarding knowledge loss as it pertains to national security when baby boom employees depart. The researcher provided a summary of the research methods, instruments, and the process followed for data collection and evaluation to address the research questions. The phenomenological method relied on observing the participant and phenomenon under study, including the researcher's experience in data collection and analysis (Simon, 2006).

Research Questions

In qualitative research, the review of the research literature plays a role in contextualizing the research question (Shank, 2006). In contrast, quantitative research questions are designed to verify and predict (Shank, 2006). Phenomenologist will describe the phenomena under study through descriptive interviews to articulate the experience of the industrial security managers and security specialists (Giorgi, 2009). In comparison, qualitative research questions lead the audience to gaining a deeper understanding of the phenomena (Shank, 2006). The research questions were directed to the participants' lived experiences and feelings toward knowledge sharing in an industrial security organization (Groenewald, 2004). Qualitative research interview questions are open-ended, general questions eliciting meaning about the phenomenon under study. The four qualitative research questions focused on the human experiences of the research participants (Van Manen, 2014).

In this study, the research questions explored knowledge loss and organizational readiness when industrial security managers and security specialists retire. The qualitative research questions revealed a deeper understanding of knowledge sharing in an industrial security organization. The research questions were exploratory in nature, because the research community may not have a clear image of what is going on in the industrial security organization. The interview question design is based on the researcher's work history as an industrial security manager and industrial security specialists with 28 years as an aerospace company employee, with 23 years in the industrial security organization. The following four research questions were the center of this qualitative study:

RQ1: What are the lived experiences of industrial security managers transferring knowledge from more senior employees to newer employees?

RQ1 is central to understanding the potential effect to national security if knowledge does not transfer from senior employees to newer employees. Industrial security managers are responsible for cultivating knowledge sharing in a budget-constrained environment. Security leaders must be creative and innovative in developing knowledge transfer opportunities among security personnel. The skills gap among retirement eligible employees could widen if security leaders ignore the warning signs. When leaders fail to incorporate knowledge sharing as a strategic objective for the company and security organization, the competitive advantage is threatened.

RQ2: What are the lived experiences of industrial security specialists transferring knowledge from more senior employees to newer employees?

RQ2 yielded meaningful knowledge transfer opportunities from older employees to multi-generational employees. The transfer of knowledge is important to organizations in sustaining a competitive advantage amid DoD budget reductions because of difficult economic conditions. Industrial security specialists are in a position to address knowledge transfer methods, such as best practices, creating a learning organization, improved processes, and cross-functional support. Industrial security specialists, deemed subject matter experts by the United Stated based aerospace company for their responsibility for managing multimillion-dollar defense programs. The industrial security subject matter experts rely on tacit knowledge, described as knowledge developed from experience and action, difficult to describe, and shared through discussion and common experiences (Kothari, Bickford, Edwards, Dobbins, & Meyer, 2011). The subject matter experts are in lead positions responsible for delivering security services across organizational boundaries.

Industrial security employee perception and experiences of knowledge sharing activities occurring in the security organization yielded valuable information toward the creation and deployment of knowledge sharing and learning among security personnel. Security leaders who do not cultivate a sharing and learning environment toward championing a knowledge management approach could face obstacles if they fail to engage, reward, or communicate with employees (O'Dell & Hubert, 2011). Leaders and managers who hoard knowledge will face difficulty in changing behaviors of less experienced and unmotivated employees. RQ2 provided the researcher with first-hand observations of factors that could contribute to effective knowledge sharing within a security organization.

RQ3: What lived experiences prevent sharing industrial security knowledge at the aerospace company?

In contrast, RQ3 industrial security leaders and managers who do not foster a knowledge sharing culture within their organization face challenges of questionable strategic goals and objectives. Industrial security personnel respond to RQ3 about the factors not associated with knowledge sharing in their organization. Participant responses provided leaders with recommendations toward creating and improving knowledge sharing opportunities in an industrial security organization. Furthermore, this question identified security leaders who lack necessary skills and abilities to create knowledge sharing opportunities. Security leaders have an opportunity to identify obstacles to creating knowledge management systems necessary to capture valuable knowledge before it leaves the organization.

RQ4: What knowledge management strategies are used to ensure industrial security knowledge transfers from retiring senior employees to newer employees?

RQ4 focused on the impending retirement of senior security employees and the importance of having a robust knowledge management system in place that will identify departing employees who leave with tacit knowledge after years of working in sensitive positions in the safeguarding of classified information critical to national security. RQ4 provided participant perspectives on organizational strategies designed to transfer knowledge from retiring employee to newer employees. Therefore, RQ4 provided an outline for the creation of knowledge management systems necessary to fill the skill gaps from departing older workers to remaining multi-generational employees. Security leaders possess transferrable critical security knowledge to younger employees poised to take over when Baby Boomers depart the organization and to sustain a competitive advantage among similar aerospace companies.

Research Method and Design Appropriateness.

According to Ball and Gotsill (2011), "In 2008, about 26 percent of aerospace workers became eligible for retirement" (p. 8). The researcher provided rationale for selecting the phenomenological research method to examine knowledge sharing by Baby Boomer industrial security managers and security specialists. The characteristics of the qualitative research allow the use of a range of evidence and discovery of new issues in the industrial security organization. The phenomenological researcher solicited answers to the research questions regarding the capture and sharing of tacit knowledge in the aerospace industry, by documenting lived experiences of 20 industrial security professionals. According to Thomas and Magilvy (2011), "Rigor is useful for establishing consistency of the study methods over time and provides an accurate representation of the population studied" (p. 151). The phenomenological researcher is concerned with interpreting the participants lived experiences associated with knowledge sharing in an aerospace company.

Phenomenology started with German mathematician Edward Husserl who emphasized experiences as the living of life (van Manen, 2014). The phenomenological design allows understanding and interpretation of interview responses from Baby Boomer industrial security professionals. Procedures or terms are not standardized; they are revealed via reading reports or through trial and error. In this methodology, analysis can review in a straight line, backward, or sideways before moving forward, focusing on the phenomenon under study (Thomas & Magilvy, 2011). The differences between assumptions of social life will have different research objectives. Qualitative researchers examine words and sentences in exploration of a particular phenomenon or experience toward building further knowledge (Neuman, 2003). Qualitative researchers conduct detailed examinations of the cases that offer a social-historical perspective. Researcher observation and discussion with participants provides an interpretation of experiences toward knowledge sharing. The qualitative research style provides a deep and rich focus on the topic throughout the study (Neuman, 2003). The flexibility of the phenomenological research methodology allows the researcher to acquire valuable data through interpretation and explanation of the participant's actions or experiences (Simon, 2006). This study's data collection compiled data through personal interviews with Baby Boomer industrial security managers and industrial security specialists.

Quantitative research is not appropriate for this research study because it relies on a sequential linear process designed to follow prescribed steps, versus a non-linear approach of qualitative research (Creswell, 2012). Quantitative research relies on a positivist approach, where the researcher is an expert in the quest to increase efficiencies of the study. Quantitative researchers collect information from many data points to generalize about the topic (Thomas & Magilvy, 2011). Qualitative researchers are not bound by restrictive data gathering techniques, allowing participants to provide personal accounts and perceptions. The quantitative researcher applies logic which is explicit, codified, and in a standardized sequence. Quantitative researchers focus on objectivity and mechanical techniques, standardized methods, measurement with numbers, and analysis of data with statistics that can stand up to academic rigor. In this method, quantitative research eliminates the human factor relying more on the rule of law.

The interpretive phenomenological research methodology was a suitable design for this study because it described the lived experiences of industrial security managers and industrial security specialists tasked with creating knowledge management systems and motivating employees to share knowledge in an industrial security organization. Mills and Smith (2011) contended that investments in knowledge management initiatives could improve organizational effectiveness. The researcher is passionate about the study as it pertains to knowledge sharing in an industrial security organization given impending Baby Boomer retirements and the potential loss of knowledge to competitors. The phenomenological method is the most appropriate research method because the researcher will interpret security manager's experiences regarding sharing and transferring knowledge in an aerospace company, without his personal biases. A phenomenologist's primary concern is with understanding lived experiences of participants, rather than how researchers conceptualize, theorize, categorize, or reflect on the phenomenon (Given, 2008). Data preconceptions were bracketed to ensure the lived experiences of the research participants emerged. The phenomenological methodology selection because it involves an informal process using semi-structured, open-ended interview questions to evoke an honest and authentic response from research participant's experiences (Moustakas, 1994).

In contrast, quantitative methods including correlational and experimental designs are not appropriate for providing perspective or interpretation of research experiences. A quantitative research approach was not suitable for this study because it eliminates the human factor. Quantitative research stresses objectivity and relies on mechanical techniques making. In quantitative research, perspective and interpretation are perceived as liabilities; however, qualitative researchers acknowledge interpretation is inevitable (Shank, 2006). The interactive methods of qualitative research are subjective reflecting the experiences, values and biases of the researcher (Szyjka, 2012). The phenomenological researcher desires to understand the consciousness of the participant involved in the study. Giorgi (2009) posited, "The reason phenomenology is often associated with qualitative research practices in this era of science is that it is a philosophy that offers a certain logic for legitimizing qualitative discriminations with rigor" (p. 5).

The social sciences such as sociology, psychology, and ethnography offer explanation while phenomenology describes and interprets (Van Manen, 2014). A mixed-method design was not used because quantitative data elements are not appropriate for this research study, opposed to qualitative data where open-ended interview questions will provide actual words of people (Creswell, 2012). The mixed methods approach encompasses both qualitative and quantitative data to answer the particular research question (Hesse-Biber, 2010). Employing a mixed methods design adds to the credibility and generalizability of the study by including narratives and numbers. Since ethnography includes interviews, observations, and historical research it was not conducive to obtaining participant perception and lived experiences central to a phenomenological methodology. The phenomenological study was employed to obtain participant perceptions and lived experiences of the phenomenon under study. Crowley-Henry (as cited in Hogan, Dolan, & Donnelly, 2009) expressed that ethnography is concerned with the study of a particular culture through observation contained in extensive field notes. Ethnographic inquiry is grounded in cultural anthropology with researchers conducting social science research in remote locations. Ethnography focuses on describing a particular culture in a participant-observation approach (Van Manen, 2014). However, ethnography has become an important management research method in understanding organizational culture and behavior (Goulding, 2002). Organizational ethnography offers researchers opportunity to observe work group behavior to improve efficiencies, similar to the Hawthorne effect on whether certain lighting levels affected productivity (Neyland, 2008). An ethnographic method was not selected because of the long periods required to study participants in an organizational setting. A case study strategy was not employed because the type of research questions being asked sought to identify the rich, lived experiences of each participant (Yin, 2009). The phenomenological method provided a textural account of the lived experiences and perceptions of industrial security managers and security specialists and how knowledge is shared or is not shared in an industrial security organization. The goal of this study was to derive findings that will lead to further research and findings associated with knowledge sharing in an industrial security organization (Moustakas, 1994). Sharing knowledge from Baby Boomer security managers and security specialists eligible to retire in 5 to 10 years is critical to sustaining a competitive advantage.

During the selection process, it was found that grounded theory was not suitable for this study because it is a data driven approach, which uses a systematic process of the creation of new theory from old theory (Shank, 2006). In grounded theory, researchers examine a number of participants who have experienced an action and interaction (Creswell, 2012). Originally developed by the RAND Corporation, the Delphi method consisted of three rounds of survey questions to a panel of experts who explore and refine responses to survey questions (Simon, 2006). In a Delphi study, the researcher can ask either qualitative or quantitative interview questions contrary to the qualitative interview process where the researcher will ask qualitative open-ended questions designed to evoke a response from the research questions. An ethnographic approach has its roots in anthropology where the researcher focus is on learning from members of a cultural group (Simon, 2006). Typically, researchers conduct extensive fieldwork to learn about the culture under study. The ethnographic researcher is actively involved in analyzing and interpreting a culture (Simon, 2006).

Population, Sampling Technique, and Sampling Frame

Population.

The United States-based aerospace company's S&FP organization has 1,392 personnel, which includes 550 industrial security personnel. The industrial security organization sample consisted of industrial security and government computing security personnel. However, both disciplines represent industrial security personnel within the industrial security organization. The industrial security personnel possess similar job and skill characteristics, depending on the level of experience within their job codes. The non- managers represent security specialist LAHQ 1 through LAHQ 5, with industrial security managers classified as Level-K (first line manager), Level-L (middle manager), and Level-M (senior manager). Government computing security managers and non-managers did not participate in this study.

The sample population consisted of 10

industrial security managers and 10 security specialists who were purposefully selected using the following criterion: (a) Baby Boomer industrial security managers born between 1946 and 1964, (b) Baby Boomer industrial security specialists born between 1946 and 1964, (c) a Top Secret clearance, Secret Compartmented Information (SCI) and/or Special Access Program (SAP), (d) eligible to retire from the aerospace company in 5 to 10 years, and (e) work in the Northwest, Southwest, Midwest, or Eastern regional security office of the United States-based aerospace company. The Enterprise Plant Security System (EPSS) database was available to the researcher to select the 20 industrial security professionals. The data in the EPSS repository consisted of Job Title, AEMS (Aerospace Electronic Messaging Service) Identification Number, Name, Work City, Work State, Service Year, Clearance, Special Access Program (SAP), and Secret Compartmentalized Information (SCI). The EPSS database contains personally identified information (PII) for each of the industrial security managers and security specialists. The database is an enterprise standard that is only accessible by aerospace company security personnel. Permission to use the EPSS database to obtain a purposeful sample of participants came from the Director of Security (see Appendix G). The researcher studied the sample population and generalized about the target population under study. Participants refusing to be part of the study were described as a respondent who was not willing to be interviewed and included in Chapter 4 of the dissertation. The industrial security managers possess innate knowledge and experience gained from working classified and intelligence programs at various locations of the aerospace company defense business unit.

Sampling Technique.

The researcher selected a large enough sample that will answer the research question, but not so large that the data will inhibit in-depth analysis (Draper & Swift, 2011). A purposeful sample of 10 Baby Boomer industrial security managers and 10 Baby Boomer security specialists emerged as the target population. The participants are subject matter experts (SME) in the government security organization. The selection criteria designed to identify senior level security professionals responsible for multi-billion dollar programs within the United States-based Aerospace Company. The researcher identified fully structured interviews with predefined questions administered in a preset order (Draper & Swift, 2010). In contrast, probability sampling for quantitative research was not appropriate for this qualitative study. Probability sampling allows for a preplanned approach using mathematical theory (Neuman, 2003).

The phenomenological study employed a purposeful sample where all possible cases fit particular criteria, with selection based on the judgment, and preselected participants of the security organization (Neuman, 2003). The Baby Boomer industrial security managers and industrial security specialists selected from data obtained from the EPSS database. The data in the EPSS repository includes Job Title, Aerospace Company Employee Number, Name, Work City, Work State, Service Year, Clearance, Special Access Program (SAP), and Secret Compartmentalized Information (SCI).

The study participants were selected based on the following criteria, (a) Baby Boomer industrial security managers born between 1946 and 1964, (b) Baby Boomer industrial security specialists born between 1946 and 1964, (c) a Top Secret clearance, Secret Compartmented Information (SCI) and/or Special Access Program (SAP), (d) eligible to retire from the aerospace company in 5 to 10 years, and (e) work in the Northwest, Southwest, Midwest, or Eastern regional security office of the United States-based aerospace company. Additionally, the researcher selected three industrial security managers from the Southwest region to participate in a pilot study to clarity and ensure the interview questions were accurate and relevant to the study. The researcher identified 10 industrial security managers and 10 industrial security specialists deliberately selected with the explicit purpose of identifying knowledge transfer gaps in an aerospace company (Draper & Swift, 2010).

Random samples represented the population, which is contrary to a purposeful sample (Neuman, 2003). Random sampling allows researchers to analyze the relationship between the sample and population using statistical analysis. The phenomenological design describes, analyzes, and interprets industrial security managers' and security specialists' responses to the six demographic and nine semi-structured, open-ended research questions. The selection criteria focused on security manager and industrial security specialists lived experiences and perceptions about formal and informal knowledge sharing opportunities. Failure to adhere to selection criteria could weaken the phenomenological study. The general characteristics identified participants, and the researcher was able to complete the nomination process. A process of ranking and culling contributed to the selection of industrial security managers and industrial security specialists. Researchers protect the integrity of the research by ensuring participant confidentiality, privacy, and anonymity (see Appendix H). As a research tool, the phenomenological methodology was essential for obtaining independent thought from each research participant. The research participant responses were anonymous, and feedback was controlled, with a structured information flow making the phenomenological method an appropriate research tool. These characteristics provided an advantage over traditional linear scientific based quantitative survey methodologies, which are not appropriate for this study.

Sampling Frame.

A purposeful sample of 10 industrial security managers and 10 industrial security specialists provided a sampling frame based on the following criteria, (a) Baby Boomer industrial security managers born between 1946 and 1964, (b) Baby Boomer industrial security specialists born between 1946 and 1964, (c) a Top Secret clearance, Secret Compartmented Information (SCI) and/or Special Access Program (SAP), (d) eligible to retire from the aerospace company in 5 to 10 years, and (e) work in the Northwest, Southwest, Midwest, or Eastern regional security office of the United States-based aerospace company. The researcher sought to collect data to explain the phenomenon by constructing theories (Given, 2008). The researcher gathered enough relevant information through data saturation where no new information emerges (Given, 2008). Research participants fitting these criteria received an invitation to participate in the phenomenological study. The research study objective was to identity the population sample through a purposeful sample of selected participants and to guard against presenting an unbalanced account of the phenomenon if data saturation did not occur (Given, 2008).

The phenomenological study provided an understanding of the knowledge sharing issues facing the industrial security organization through delivery of six demographic and nine semi-structured, open-ended interview questions. As a culture-sharing group, Baby Boomer industrial security managers and industrial security specialists were examined to understand the possible reluctance to share knowledge with security employees. This phenomenological research study described participant lived experiences in an industrial security organization. The six demographic and nine semi-structured, open-ended interview questions were provided to 20 industrial security professionals to solicit knowledge sharing experiences.

The phenomenological method provided the best approach for soliciting expert opinion from Baby Boomer industrial security managers and security specialists to determine management strategies, tacit knowledge capturing processes, and methods to enhance knowledge sharing in an industrial security organization. Participants' anonymity reduced study biases that could occur in traditional data collection methods. The phenomenological technique did capture opinions, experience, and knowledge of each participant. The phenomenological method allowed industrial security managers and security specialists to interpret their experiences and perceptions regarding knowledge sharing and organizational readiness when Baby Boomers retire from the industrial security organization (Simon, 2006).

Industrial security managers and specialists contributed practical experience in transferring knowledge to new employees through the creation of knowledge management systems. The interview questions converted into unambiguous questions to produce sociological data (Shank, 2006). An organization's loss of knowledge can be detrimental if not included as a corporate strategy to create effective knowledge management systems and a willingness to share knowledge among employees. Organizationally, the creation, sharing, and reusing of knowledge toward improving business opportunities are central to knowledge management (Goel, Rana, & Rastogi, 2010). The phenomenological approach provided a rigorous research method for participants to contribute anonymously by providing their expert opinion during the semi-structured, open-ended personal interviews. The phenomenological study intent was to solicit Baby Boomer security manager and security specialist perceptions and lived experiences in sharing knowledge in an industry security organization. The six demographic and nine content-related personal interview question responses were collected, analyzed, and interpreted using the QSR ATLAS.ti 7 qualitative data analysis software. Data collection occurred through personal interviews with each study participant.

The interviews were digitally recorded, transcribed, and entered data into a qualitative data analysis program designed to interpret and explain the social phenomena. The researcher reviewed and clustered each transcript into common categories, removing repetitive statements toward obtaining textural descriptions of the phenomenon and testing out the ideas about what is going on in the study

(Moustakas, 1994). After coding data, themes began to emerge central to the study (Gibbs, 2002). The outcome of the analysis provided theoretical statements responding to the research questions (Simon, 2006). Research findings consisted of a narrative discussion using tables, and demographic data to augment the discussion. The objective was to establish casual connections between the interviews and the predicted outcome toward knowledge transfer occurring within the aerospace company security organization (Gibbs, 2002). The coding method is a procedure organization of the text of the transcripts to discover patterns or themes within the organizational structure (Auerbach & Silverstein, 2003). The outcome identified knowledge transfer gaps occurring in the industrial security organization. The coding of data moved the researcher from raw text to the phenomenon under study (Auerbach & Sliverstein, 2003). A theme represents an extended phrase that identifies what a unit of data means (Saldana, 2012).

ATLAS.ti 7 assisted with managing, exploring patterns, themes, and relationships from the interview question responses from the 20 participants. The qualitative data analysis software assisted the

researcher with systematically working through the
data to identify and uncover emerging themes using
queries (Wiltshier, 2011). The qualitative data
analysis software analysis program ATLAS.ti 7 was
employed to remove unrelated sections of the
transcripts while focusing on relevant sections to
obtain an understanding of the phenomenon of the
inability to capture and share knowledge among
industrial security personnel (Goble, Austin, Larsen,
Kreitzer, & Brintnell, 2012). The advantages of open-
ended interview questions are: (a) obtaining
unanticipated answers, (b) describing real views of
the participant, and (c) participants could answer
questions in their own words (Simon, 2006). In
contrast, a survey formatted data collection technique
was not suitable for this study because it does not
provide the researcher with in-depth analysis of open-
ended semi-structured interview questions. A survey,
which was not conducive for this study, is a
quantitative process designed to identify trends in
attitudes, opinions, behaviors, and characteristics of
participants (Creswell, 2002).

The industrial security managers and industrial
security specialist's selection occurred using the

EPSS database. Solicitation of industrial security managers and security specialists occurred through a scripted e-mail to participants (see Appendix B). Industrial security personnel meeting the criteria and deciding to take part in the interview received a letter introducing (see Appendix A) and outlining the intent of the phenomenological study. Each research participant read, signed, and forwarded an informed consent agreement form (see Appendix C) prior to receiving the semi-structured, open-ended interview questions. When participants received the informed consent agreement form the researcher scheduled interview sessions. The researcher made contact with each research participant to begin the semi-structured and open-ended interview. A telephone interview schedule was communicated to research participants by the researcher because of geographic and cost constraints to attend an in-person interview. However, in-person interviews occurred with seven of the 20 participants to help obtain a profound appreciation of the phenomenon under study. The researcher requested each research participant use their personal time to participate in the in-person or telephone data collection phase to ensure compliance with company time charging regulations.

Participants must comprehend the confidentiality and anonymity of the phenomenological study. The researcher requested permission from study participants to use their personally identifiable information (PII) when purposefully selecting each participant from the EPSS system. The participants granted their consent by submitting the informed consent agreement form (see Appendix C) through the aerospace company mail system to the researcher prior to scheduling an interview. The researcher began the interview process by contacting each research participant (see Appendix D).

Prior to the selection process, all participants were provided informed consent forms indicating that PII information would only be used in the selection of three pilot study participants and the 20 main study participants. Participants read and signed the consent statement and provided their approval by affixing their signature as a voluntary participant. The interview process began with contact for each research participant (see Appendix D). The researcher ensured compliance with the interview protocol by adhering to research participant confidentiality through the coding and protection of Baby Boomer industrial security managers' and industrial security specialists' responses to the interview questions (see Appendix D).

The researcher advised participants the study could be published, but participant names would not be used. The naming convention used for the study participants was: (a) Baby Boomer industrial security managers (M1-M10.), and (b) Baby Boomer security specialists (S1-S10). All printed hard-copy consent forms were stored and secured in a locked filing system to be shredded at the conclusion of three years time.

The researcher provided each study participant with information pertaining to the research study, and the process to protect his or her personally identifiable information (PII). The researcher generated and assigned random numbers to each Baby Boomer study participant to ensure anonymity. Each Baby Boomer industrial security manager received a random generated designator beginning with Manager 1 (M1) through Manager (M10), and Specialist 1 (S1) through Specialist (S10) in the

identification of industrial security specialists. The
geographic location of the industrial security
managers represented security offices in the
Northwest, Southwest, Midwest, and Eastern regions
of the United States, which made the telephone
interviews an essential and optimal component
toward capturing security personnel lived experiences
and perceptions. The researcher digitally recorded
participant interviews and uploaded each directly to
the researcher's personal computer.

An advantage of telephone interviews is the
ability to communicate across multiple locations,
where participants can participate without incurring
travel and costs constraints in a budget conscious
environment. The interviewer needed to listen, stay
engaged and interested, suspend judgment, and
probe participants for more depth concerning the
research question (Draper & Swift, 2010). The
telephone interviews provided optimum
communication for participants located in four regions
of the county, eliminating direct contact with the
participants. Inclusion of 10 in-person interviews
strengthened the data collection phase of this study.
Irvine (2011) posited there were no empirically based

comparisons between face-to-face and telephone interview methods. The researcher relied on the EPSS database system for selecting the phenomenological study participants.

The Baby Boomer industrial security managers and industrial security specialists were purposefully selected using the following criteria: (a) Baby Boomer industrial security managers born between 1946 and 1964, (b) Baby Boomer industrial security specialists born between 1946 and 1964, (c) a Top Secret clearance, Secret Compartmented Information (SCI) and Special Access Program (SAP), (d) eligible to retire from the aerospace company in 5 to 10 years, and (e) work in the Northwest, Southwest, Midwest, or Eastern regional security office of the United States-based aerospace company. Data for the phenomenological research study were collected using semi-structured, open-ended interview questions allowing individuals to respond truthfully to the interview questions (see Appendix D). The sample population received an electronic mail invitation to participate in the interview process administered for a purposeful sample of 20 industrial security managers and security specialists. The data was analyzed, coded, and summarized for the 20 participant interviews using the ATLAS.ti 7 qualitative data analysis software. Each study participant was allotted one hour maximum to provide answers for the 15 interview questions. Each participant identified a location free of interruptions to complete the semi-structured, open-ended interview questions. Study participants used their personal time to participate in the in-person or telephone interview during the data collection phase to ensure compliance with government contractual obligations and compliance with company time charging regulations. The instrumentation methodology was essential to the research study accuracy.

A researcher develops explanations or generalizations from the data collected as it pertains to the interview responses. In this study, the data was analyzed and categorized into clusters and themes designed to interpret participant experiences. Data analysis consisted of a rank ordered scoring of responses from the interview questions regarding the possible reluctance to share knowledge strategies in an industrial security organization. This phenomenological research study addressed one cultural group in an industrial security organization regarding perceptions and lived experiences of knowledge sharing. The exploratory design allowed the researcher to gather qualitative data in examining the research phenomenon to explain the relationship found in the qualitative data. The phenomenological study consisted of an analysis of themes, patterns, and relationships obtained from the interview question responses. The research analysis and output yielded a transformation of the raw text of the interview transcripts into a theoretical narrative (Auerbach & Silverstein, 2003).

Theming the data and coding required reflection on research participant meanings and outcomes regarding the topic under investigation (Saldana, 2009). The phenomenological researcher presents the study through qualitative data collection obtained from semi-structured, open-ended personal interviews with Baby Boomer industrial security managers and security specialist. The researcher used the qualitative data analysis software to organize and manage participant interviews (Gibbs, 2002). The researcher captured and interpreted the findings that confirmed and contradicted the researcher's personally held beliefs (Gibbs, 2002). After data was examined, coded, and interpreted, the outcomes addressed the research questions under study. Research findings were presented in a narrative discussion in which the author summarizes the findings from the data analysis (Creswell, 2008). The researcher reported research findings using figures that show the connection among themes to include a demographic table (Creswell, 2008). The following chronological steps represented the data collection process the researcher followed.

1. Purposefully selected three pilot and 20 research study participants using EPSS database.
2. Sent letter of introduction to three purposefully selected pilot study Baby Boomer industrial security managers.
3. Provided an informed consent agreement to three pilot study participants.
4. The pilot study was completed within three business days.
5. Reviewed and incorporated pilot study's recommendations.
6. Utilized EPSS database to identify Baby Boomer

security managers and security specialists.

7. Sent letter of introduction to participants.

8. Identified 20 participants (10 industrial security managers, and 10 industrial security specialists).

9. Provided solicitation script to 20 participants.

10. Sent informed consent agreement form to 20 participants.

11. Scheduled one-hour time slots for personal interviews with 20 participants representing Northwest, Southwest, Midwest, and Eastern regional security offices.

12. Began personal interview process (telephone and in-person) with each research participant.

13. Digitally recorded interviews.

14. Transcribed personal interviews using ATLAS.ti 7 data analysis software program, and conducted qualitative data analysis searching for patterns, themes, and relations of narrative data.

Instrumentation

Qualitative research occurs through data collection, analysis, and interpretation of narrative response toward capturing the complexities of a problem (Creswell, 2012). As an example, unreliable data can occur if questions are unclear, or if participants do not understand questions (Creswell, 2012). Data was collected employing semi-structured, open-ended personal interview questions. A primary step of the phenomenological study required long interviews to collect data on the research questions (Moustakas, 1994). The research interviews were conducted within an informal and relaxed atmosphere for the participant to respond openly and honestly. The researcher conducted personal interviews with 10 industrial security managers and 10 industrial security specialists to relate experiences into patterns and themes to better understand knowledge sharing in an industrial security organization.

In phenomenological methodology, the researcher is the recording instrument to see how the participants interpret their worlds and how the researcher can interpret their interpretations (Shank, 2006). Prior to initiating interview, the researcher provided a letter of introduction (see Appendix A) to explain the study and to solicit research participation. Participants had a prescribed time limit of one hour to complete the telephone or in-person interview questions. The six demographic and nine personal interview questions were included (see Appendix D). The informed consent agreement form was included (see Appendix C) in the correspondence. The interviews were digitally recorded and transcribed for each participant. A digital recording of the interview instead of note taking enabled the analysis of relevant data from participants. Interview transcripts were provided to participants for evaluation and consent prior to the inclusion of the qualitative data to achieve higher internal validity. Changes to the interview questions occurred only during the pilot study. The participants were not allowed to change their answers after the interviews.

Instrumentation Validity.

Validity refers to the extent of differences found with a measuring instrument that reflect the acceptability and persuade-ability of a study (Van Manen, 2014). In qualitative interviews, the interviewed participants were asked open-ended questions, and the interviewer listened to, and recorded responses (Creswell, 2012). A research study with high internal validity translates into a study with few errors while a study with low internal validity means errors are likely (Neuman, 2003). The validity of the personal interview questions correlated to the relationship to the research questions of knowledge sharing and organizational readiness when Baby Boomer industrial security managers and industrial security specialists retire. The importance of administering effective open-ended questions evoked deeper and detailed responses from the participants. The interview questions were applicable to all of the industrial security managers and industrial security specialists. The pilot study strengthened the instrument validity by improving the accuracy and clarity of the interview questions before dissemination to the participants. The phenomenological technique provided confirmation phases from the extraction of themes and patterns to establish relationships to the research questions. An emphasis on honesty was stressed in the observation and documentation of participant perspectives and was part of the explicit record (Shank, 2006).

Qualitative studies that can generalize results to a wide population are concerned with external validity (Leighton, 2010). For example, if a study was created in a laboratory or with a particular group of participants, researchers want to know if the study can be generalized (Neuman, 2003). A research study exhibiting high external validity suggests study results can be generalized across populations, where low external validity suggests results can be applied to a specific target population (Leighton, 2010). The interview sample size of 10 Baby Boomer industrial security managers and 10 industrial security specialists, across four geographic regions, contributed to high external validity and the capability of the researcher to generalize the study (Neuman, 2003). The use of purposeful sampling using the EPSS system contributes to the selection of qualified and experienced industrial security managers and industrial security specialists who have direct experience in knowledge sharing activities. The use of the database analysis software, ATLAS.ti 7, contributed to the validity of the study in the storing, coding, analysis, and interpretation of the data.

Instrumentation Reliability.

The reliability of this study depended on qualitative research generating theories that explain phenomena in the world (Nicholls, 2009). The phenomenological researcher is concerned with the dependability of the study to describe the social and personal phenomena occurring in similar aerospace organizations. The goal and objectives of the researcher were to produce consistent and reliable measurements (Shank, 2006). The interview questions and responses provided accurate data to provided a picture of phenomena under study. The coding system, using ATLAS.ti 7 delivered an accurate and consistent measurement of the data collected from the personal interview questions.

Instrumentation Pilot Testing.

A pilot study consisted of three industrial security managers representing the Southwest regional security office before the researcher administers the six demographic and nine semi-structured interview questions to the study participants. The pilot study participants were selected based on the following research criteria from the EPSS database: (a) Baby Boomer industrial security managers born between 1946 and 1964, (b) Baby Boomer industrial security specialists born between 1946 and 1964, (c) a Top Secret clearance, Secret Compartmented Information (SCI) and Special Access Program (SAP), (d) eligible to retire from the aerospace company in 5 to 10 years, and (e) work in the Northwest, Southwest, Midwest, or Eastern regional security office of the United States-based aerospace company. The three pilot study participants received the informed consent agreement (see Appendix C) form prior to dissemination of the telephone, and in-person interview questions.

The pilot study provided a warning the research study could fail if rules weren't followed, and/or research questions are inappropriate (Simon, 2006). The pilot study provided interview question accuracy, consistency, and dependability. The pilot study assisted the refinement of the research study and the researcher with drawing conclusions about the potential effect on research participant responses to the interview questions. The comments received from the three pilot study participants helped evaluate the instrument. The researcher coded and categorized participant responses of repetitive patterns (Saldana, 2009). The pilot study participants did not take part in the final study. The pilot study allowed a review of decisions prior to the main study, to include study preparedness before moving forward to the main study (Duma et al., 2009). The pilot study completed within three business days to accommodate study completion timeline. Results from the pilot study were included in Chapter 4 of this dissertation.

Informed Consent and Confidentiality.

The researcher contacted the purposeful sample population of 10 industrial security managers and 10 security specialists through company electronic mail system using the Solicitation Script (see Appendix B) to describe the intent of the study and solicit participation. If the research study participants did not want to participate in the study after receiving the solicitation script, they could respond to the researcher through company electronic mail system. A lack of response signified approval to participate. Each industrial security manager and security specialists received a letter of introduction (see Appendix A) explaining the intent of the phenomenological study through company electronic mail. Prior to starting the interviews, each research participant signed a consent form (see Appendix C) to take part in the study before the interview occurred. The researcher provided the informed consent form to 20 study participants through company electronic mail. Upon completion of the Informed Consent Form, the participants mailed the signed document to the researcher in a company transmittal envelope to the following mail code: H012-A207. Because the informed consent and interviewing took place separately, and because the participant's information was coded to assure anonymity, there is no direct connection or link between the informed consent and the interviewee survey questionnaire.

The participants were advised of the withdrawal procedure, including no penalty for withdrawing before, during, or after the administration of the study concluded. All research documentation was immediately destroyed when or if a participant withdraws from the study. All electronic files and all hard copy information would be destroyed if a participant removed themself from the study, and would not be part of the data analysis. When participants returned the informed consent forms the researcher scheduled in-person and telephone interviews with participants. Participants' interview questions were alpha-numerically coded to ensure confidentiality during distribution.

Participant informed consent agreement forms were signed, received, and filed by the researcher before the interviews commenced. The face-to-face and telephone interviews took place at the regional security offices of the aerospace company, located in the Northwest, Southwest, Midwest, and Eastern regions of the country. The researcher advised each participant to use his or her personal time for the interview. Participants working on a government contract are prohibited from charging personal time for this interview. Participants received a copy of the interview questions (see Appendix D) before the personal interviews occurred.

The confidentiality and anonymity of each

research participant ensured research credibility and integrity. The researcher requested highly restricted data obtained from the EPSS database from the director of security for use in the phenomenological study (see Appendix G). Personally identifiable information (PII) obtained from the EPSS database, was protected during each phase of the study. Company policy prohibits the use of highly sensitive PII data, which can only be accessed in a secure work environment by industrial security personnel. Participant names did not appear in this study. Each participant's name was coded (M1 through M10 for managers, and S1 through S10 for industrial security specialists) to ensure confidentiality of each study participant. Any findings that would reveal the researcher's identity were destroyed (Shank, 2006). The data collected was stored in a locked cabinet for a period of three years; access to the information will be restricted to the researcher. After the three years from the conclusion of the study, all hardcopy and electronic data was destroyed.

The researcher created a master list consisting of participant names with alpha numeric coding of each participant (M1-M-10, S1-S10).

The researcher administered six demographic, and nine content-related, semi-structured, open-ended interview questions to the sample of 20 Baby Boomer industrial security managers and security specialists located at the United States-based aerospace company with security offices located in the Northwest, Southwest, Midwest, and Eastern regions of the country. A modified van Kaam technique of data analysis was essential to the phenomenological study (as cited in Moustakas, 1994). Prior to beginning the data collection process the researcher obtained required permissions as part of the informed consent process in protecting the anonymity of each research participant.

Data Analysis and Measurement.

Qualitative analysis of the narrative data was collected to develop relationships between themes, patterns, and relationships central to the research study. Quantitative data analysis focuses on statistical analysis interpreted in a numerical format opposed to a narrative format. The interpretive phenomenological method was necessary for interpreting the lived experiences of the 20 industrial security managers and security specialists of the selected aerospace company. The lived experiences of the security professionals provided rich exploration into their day-to-day activities in a complex work environment. The ATLAS.ti 7 qualitative data analysis software application was used to organize text, graphics, audio and visual data fields, in addition to coding, memos, and findings (Creswell, 2012).

Prior to using the qualitative data analysis software required introductory training in ATLAS.ti 7 to understand what the program offered. ATLAS.ti 7 offered the researcher the ability to manage and organize data, ideas, querying data, modeling ideas and concepts, and reporting (Bergin, 2011). ATLAS.ti 7 stored, coded, analyzed, and sorted data collected for the phenomenological study. The qualitative data analysis software provided a wide range of applications to process the research data. The process of coding data occurs during data collection, in order to determine what data to collect next (Creswell, 2012). Coding the data in ATLAS.ti 7 involved the creation of nodes, which are a collection of references about themes, places, people, or other

areas of interest to the researcher (Bergin, 2011).
Themes emerged and were coded or labeled to
condense the mass of data associated with the 15
interview questions designed to describe the
phenomena.

The process of coding is dependent on the
how the research questions, text, data, can be
organized into small categories of information which
will be used to write the narrative (Creswell, 2012).
For example, reports were created to identify
aerospace company security managers (M1) and
industrial security specialists (S1) responses to each
interview question. The researcher filtered out
personal points of view, clearly identifying the
concepts, cluster of meaning units, summarizing each
interview, and makes a composite summary (Shank,
2006). Code words were created and assigned for
each research participant. ATLAS.ti 7 software
automatically numbers text and formats the files;
however, the researcher interpreted interview findings
to formulate patterns and themes. The large amount
of interviewing text was assigned a coding structure to
interpret the data and identify themes. Another
advantage of using ATLAS.ti 7 was the ability to

import digitally recorded interviews, which were transcribed and referenced in this study (Bergin, 2011). ATLAS.ti 7 helped to code words, run analyses for inclusion into Chapter 5, and has the ability to note trends in the interpretation of participant answers to the semi-structured, open-ended interview questions. The researcher identified whether significant statements *textural descriptions* are (what happened) or *structural descriptions* (how it was experienced) to convey an overall substance of the experience (Creswell, 2012).

The interviews were transcribed and analyzed using Moustakas' (1994) modified van Kaam process that included the following:

1. Listing and Preliminary Grouping.
2. Reduction and Elimination.
3. Clustering and Theming the Invariant Constituents.
4. Final Identification of the Invariant Constituents and Themes by Application: Validation.
5. Individual Textural Description.
6. Individual Structural Description.
7. Textural-Structural Description of the meanings

and essences of the experiences.

8. Composite description of meanings, and essences of experience. (Moustakas, 1994)

Furthermore, the exclusion of repetitive and vague experiences is consistent with van Kaam's methodology. If the themes were not explicit, compatible, or relevant to the participants' experiences, they were eliminated from the study (Moustakas, 1994).

Presentation of Study Findings.

The study findings using lists, tables, and graphs that represented themes and patterns identified in the personal interviews. The phenomenological study focus was on the research questions that concentrated on meaning and themes from participant interviews (Moustakas, 1994). The research questions were central to the prioritization of themes that provided the researcher with a vital, rich, and textured study. The cross sectional interviews provided rich and insightful patterns for interpretation by the researcher (Shank, 2006). Prioritization of knowledge sharing, motivation, and knowledge management were central to the research study. The graphs provided a pictorial representation of the main themes and patterns that emerged from the personal interviews. A breakout of centralized themes provided a graphical representation of participant responses from each of the four regional security offices. The research study's focus was on the following themes: (a) Knowledge Management Systems, (b) Knowledge Sharing, Knowledge Transfer, (c) Knowledge Gaps, (d) Motivation to Share Knowledge, and (e) Reluctance to Share Knowledge.

The researcher performed data analysis by transcribing the interviews and importing the information into ATLAS.ti 7 for initial coding, which is the selection of important groups of statements from each interview response (Cane, McCarthy, & Halawi, 2010). Themes emerged from describing and organizing possible observations toward comprehending the phenomenon (Saldana, 2009). The themes consisted of participant statements and ideas that emerged from the interviews to address knowledge transfer among security professionals at the aerospace company (Saldana, 2009). The tables

were constructed for each of the steps in the modified
van Kaam model. The themes were extrapolated from
participants' interviews, which translated into the
findings synthesized using tables and integrated into
the seven phases of van Kaam's model.

Summary

The interpretive phenomenological study was
employed to determine perceptions and individual
experiences of Baby Boomer security managers' and
security specialists' responsibility of knowledge
sharing and organizational readiness when security
employees begin to retire. Research methods and
design appropriateness focused on the semi-
structured, open-ended interview process designed to
describe security managers' and security specialists'
lived experiences of knowledge sharing and
organizational readiness when Baby Boomers retire.
The sample population was industrial security
managers and industrial security specialists dispersed
in the Northwest, Southwest, Midwest, and Eastern
regions of the country. The researcher employed a
purposeful sample of 10 industrial security managers

and 10 industrial security specialists to take part in the study. Semi-structured, open-ended interviews were necessary to evoke discussion regarding knowledge sharing and organizational readiness when Baby Boomer security managers and industrial security specialists retire. Data analysis and measurement were conducted using the qualitative data analysis software ATLAS.ti 7 to manage and organize data, ideas, querying, modeling, and reporting of the findings.

The phenomenological technique began with pre-selected items deployed through a pilot study to three industrial security managers who provided feedback on interview instrument clarity and accuracy. The phenomenological technique was the optimal method for the study because it provided a profound understanding of knowledge sharing methods and strategies in an industrial security organization. The interview questions were designed to solicit individual experiences of security managers and security specialists based on the following criteria: (a) Baby Boomer industrial security managers born between 1946 and 1964, (b) Baby Boomer industrial security specialist born between 1946 and

1964, (c) a Top Secret clearance, Secret Compartmented Information (SCI) and/or Special Access Program (SAP), (d) eligible to retire from the aerospace company in 5 to 10 years, and (e) work in the Northwest, Southwest, Midwest, or Eastern regional security office of the United States-based aerospace company.

The phenomenological methodology provided an efficient method for capturing input from geographically dispersed study participants located in four regions of the United States. Purposeful sampling ensured the inclusion of a qualified and experienced panel of experts who contributed to a robust study. Data collection occurred through nine semi-structured, open-ended, personal interview questions to 10 industrial security managers and 10 security specialists representing security professionals from the United States-based aerospace company. The researcher employed a modified version of the van Kaam method to evaluate the research data (Moustakas, 1994). The use of Baby Boomer industrial security managers and industrial security specialists added to a collaborative research study that examined knowledge creation and sharing opportunities in the industrial security organization. Participants were informally asked if they would like to be part of knowledge transfer/sharing activities. However, a knowledge management initiative was undertaken prior to the completion of this study. The KM initiative is in process now, to include Knowledge Transfer tools, etc. The part two would be the creation and implementation phase of the KM program.

The participants, including the pilot study participants, completed an informed consent agreement form to ensure ethical conduct in qualitative research. The standardized consent form ensures consistent rights across all participants. The research study ensured no harm and was open, honest, and careful to ensure the confidentiality of each research participant (Shank, 2006). Participants could pull out of the research study at any time without consequences. All research documentation was destroyed immediately if a subject withdrew from the study. The researcher deleted all electronic files, and hard copy information would be destroyed. Any participants who removed themselves from the study were not part of the data analysis. After three years, the researcher destroyed all study data and deleted all electronic files to delete traces of any files.

Chapter 4 of the study included detailed research findings, and data analyses. The research design and methodology was revealed in Chapter 4. The researcher provided a demographic table representing the 10 industrial security managers and 10 security specialists selected for this study. The researcher included a demographic summary to include the following: age, gender, and education. The next section of Chapter 4 provided findings from the six demographic and nine semi-structured, open-ended, interview question responses from the 20 industrial security managers. The data were analyzed for themes and were presented based on the most important topics in the data (Simon, 2006).

Major themes of significance, accounting for similar responses, were examined and findings were presented in Chapter 4. Outlier responses, where only a few of the participants replied to a research question, yielded a significant theme for the study, and were included in Chapter 4. A summary of the major themes from each participant was included in the next section.

CHAPTER IV

FINDINGS

The purpose for conducting this interpretive phenomenological research study was to examine the individual experiences of industrial security managers and industrial security specialists regarding the potential loss of organizational knowledge when Baby Boomer industrial security personnel begin to retire. In addition, to determine organizational readiness toward capturing and sharing this knowledge within the United Stated based aerospace company. The United States-based aerospace company industrial security personnel work in an environment of secrecy in the protection of national security. A purposeful sample of 20 Baby Boomer industrial security managers and industrial security specialists was central to this study. The research incorporated 20 telephone and face-to-face interviews with industrial security managers and industrial security specialists. The emphasis in Chapter 1 was to introduce the study. Chapter 2 included a review of the literature supporting the phenomenological study of knowledge occurring when older workers depart the security organization.

Chapter 3 included a discussion on the research methods and design appropriateness, population, sampling, data collection, and the validity and reliability of the phenomenological methodology. Additionally, data was collected using a semi-structured, open-ended personal face-to-face and telephone interviews with 20 participants. Personal interviews converted to digitally recording and transcribed by the researcher. A qualitative data analysis software program, ATLAS.ti 7, was used to store, code, analyze, and sort data collected for the phenomenological study. A pilot study was conducted, consisting of digitally recorded telephone and face-to-face interviews with three industrial security managers to determine the accuracy and clarity of the interview questions. Four research questions were generated to explore knowledge loss and organizational readiness when Baby Boomer industrial security personnel begin to retire. The research findings from the data collected from the industrial security managers and industrial security specialists face-to-face and telephone interviews based on research questions presented to each participant wre revealed in this chapter.

Chapter 4 included the following findings: the research methods, research questions, pilot study, sample population and demographics, epoché, instrumentation, data collection, and analysis, data analysis, modified van Kaam method of analysis, data saturation, outliers, and concluded with a chapter summary.

Research Method

An interpretive phenomenological methodology was suitable for this study because the participants lived individual experiences and perceptions can determine the essence of the phenomenon (Giorgi, 2009). The interpretive phenomenological study offered a first-hand account of research participant experiences leading to a rich description of the phenomenon (Moustakas, 1994). Interpretive phenomenological questions explored the meaning of the phenomena of knowledge sharing in the industrial security organization (Van Manen, 2014).

Participants meeting the following criteria were purposefully selected for this study, (a) Baby Boomer industrial security managers born between 1946 and 1964, (b) Baby Boomer industrial security specialists born between 1946 and 1964, (c) a Top Secret clearance, Secret Compartmented Information (SCI) and/or Special Access Program (SAP), (d) eligible to retire from the aerospace company in 5 to 10 years, and (e) work in the Northwest, Southwest, Midwest, or Eastern regional security office of a United States-based aerospace company.

A purposeful sample of 10 industrial security managers and 10 industrial security specialists employed within the aerospace company security organization participated in the study. Industrial security managers and industrial security specialists, Level 5 personnel, who were Generation X and Y employees were excluded from participating in this study. The phenomenological study focus was on the researcher obtaining concrete descriptions of the phenomenon, transforming each meaning unit into expressions of the phenomenon (Giorgi & Giorgi, 2008). The study's significance was important to the aerospace company's competitiveness in capturing future classified DoD contracts and international business. The study could benefit similar aerospace companies with creating and understanding knowledge sharing obstacles and recommendations to avert knowledge loss when Baby Boomers begin to retire. The study provided the aerospace company's security fire and protection leaders with realistic observations of managers and non-managers' willingness to share knowledge.

Research Questions.

The main research questions for this study focused on manager and non-manager perceptions and lived experiences toward knowledge sharing in an industrial security organization. Twenty face-to-face and telephone interviews were conducted of industrial security managers and industrial security specialists, Level 5 employees to help answer four principal questions central to the research question of potential knowledge loss and organizational readiness when Baby Boomer security personnel retire.

RQ1: What are the lived experiences of industrial security managers transferring knowledge from more senior employees to newer employees?

RQ2: What are the lived experiences of industrial security specialists transferring knowledge from more senior employees to newer employees?

RQ3: What lived experiences prevent sharing industrial security knowledge at the aerospace company?

RQ4: What knowledge management strategies are used to ensure industrial security knowledge transfers from retiring senior employees to newer employees?

Pilot Study.

The implementation of a pilot study included three industrial security managers, each with more than 15 years of experience as industrial security managers and professional experience to help clarify and calibrate the interview research questions. The pilot study participants were not part of the main research study and were coded P-M1 to P-M3 to ensure privacy and anonymity. Research participant P-M1 suggested a rephrasing of content question number four: In your experience, please describe how the transfer of tacit knowledge (non-codified processes) is important to sustaining a competitive advantage in the industrial security organization? Interview question four originally stated the following: In your experience, why is transferring tacit knowledge (noncodified processes) to less experienced personnel important to the industrial security organization? The rephrasing of content question four helped to clarify the interview question for the main study participants. Table 2 below represents the demographic data associated with the pilot study managers.

Table 1 - Pilot Study Managers: Demographics.

Code	Region	Gender	Years of Professional Experience	Years of Experience as a Security Manager	Level of Education
P-M1	SWR	M	15+	15+	MA
P-M2	SWR	F	15+	15+	AA
P-M3	SWR	M	15+	15+	MA

n = 3

Sample Population and Demographics.

The sample population consisted of 10 industrial security managers and 10 security specialists who were purposefully selected using the following criteria: (a) Baby Boomer industrial security managers born between 1946 and 1964, (b) Baby Boomer industrial security specialists born between 1946 and 1964, (c) a Top Secret clearance, Secret Compartmented Information (SCI) and/or Special Access Program (SAP), (d) eligible to retire from the aerospace company in 5 to 10 years, and (e) work in the Northwest, Southwest, Midwest, or Eastern regional security office of the United States-based aerospace company. Prior to the interviews, the researcher used the Enterprise Plant Security System (EPSS) database to select the 20 industrial security professionals.

The data in the EPSS repository is comprised of Job Title, AEMS (Aerospace Electronic Messaging Service) Identification Number, Name, Work City, Work State, Service Year, Clearance, Special Access Program (SAP), and Secret Compartmentalized Information (SCI). The EPSS database contains personally identified information (PII) for each of the industrial security managers and industrial security specialists. The database is an enterprise standard that is only accessible by aerospace company security personnel. Table 3 below describes the regional representation of the industrial security managers and industrial security specialists who participated in this study.

Table 2 - Participants: Demographics.

Code	Region	Gender	Years of Professional Experience	Years of Experience as a Security Manager	Level of Education	Title
M1	Southwest	M	> 15	> 15	BA	Manager
M2	Midwest	M	> 15	> 15	BA	Manager
M3	Southwest	F	> 15	> 15	BA	Manager
M4	Midwest	M	6 - 10	6 - 10	BS	Manager
M5	Midwest	M	> 15	> 15	BA	Manager
M6	Midwest	F	> 15	> 15	MS	Manager
M7	Southwest	M	> 15	> 15	AA	Manager
M8	Eastern	M	> 15	> 15	BS	Manager
M9	Eastern	M	> 15	> 15	BS	Manager
M10	Southwest	F	> 15	> 15	BS	Manager
S1	Southwest	M	> 15	> 15	MA	Security Specialist

Code	Region	Gender	Years of Professional Experience	Years of Experience as a Security Manager	Level of Education	Title
S1	Southwest	M	> 15	> 15	MA	Security Specialist
S2	Southwest	M	> 15	6 - 10	None	Security Specialist
S3	Southwest	F	6 - 10	6 - 10	BS	Security Specialist
S4	Northwest	M	> 15	6 - 10	BA	Security Specialist
S5	Midwest	M	> 15	> 15	MA	Security Specialist
S6	Southwest	M	> 15	0 - 5	AA	Security Specialist
S7	Southwest	M	> 15	6 - 10	MS	Security Specialist
S8	Southwest	M	> 15	0 - 5	MS	Security Specialist
S9	Midwest	M	> 15	> 15	AA	Security Specialist
S10	Midwest	M	> 15	0 - 5	BS	Security Specialist

n = 20

Permission to use the EPSS database to obtain a purposeful sample of participants came from the director of government security (see Appendix G); however, this data was not used in the study.

Epoché.

The researcher refrained from introducing personal knowledge and experiences during the face-to-face and telephone interviews. The bracketing of past knowledge did not allow for any pre-suppositions about the phenomenon being investigated (Giorgi, 2009). As an industrial security manager with 28 years' experience at the United States-based aerospace company, it was difficult at times not to interject personal experiences during the course of the interviews. The researcher's awareness and use of bracketing of past experience helped to keep the focus on the present research, which was essential to obtaining a new perspective of the phenomenon under study (Creswell, 2012).

Additional participant demographic information consisted of gender representation since the industrial security organization was a male dominated career field during the researcher's 28 years of employment with the company. Figure 2 below describes the gender distribution among the participants.

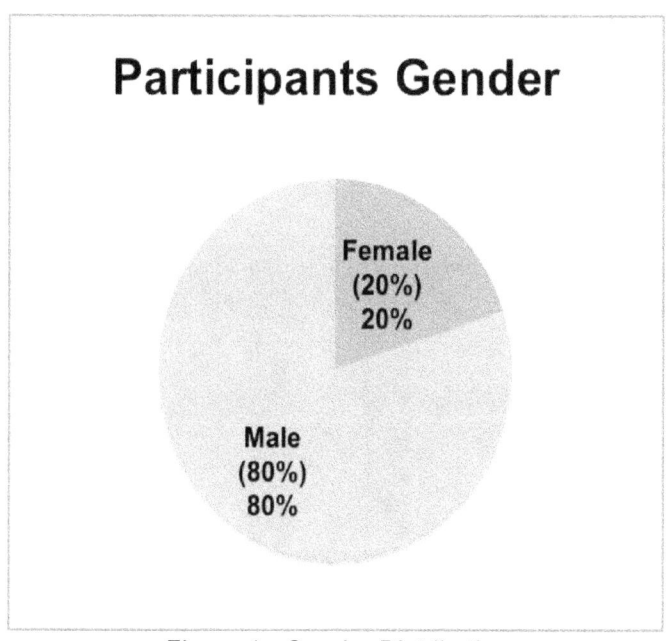

Figure 1 - Gender Distribution

With a surplus of new government contracts in the early 1980s the hiring of industrial security personnel having military or, law enforcement backgrounds were the norm during this period.

The educational data below in Figure 3 suggested a normal distribution of Bachelor, Associate, and Master's degrees among industrial security participants, with one individual not having a college degree.

Number of Participants = 20

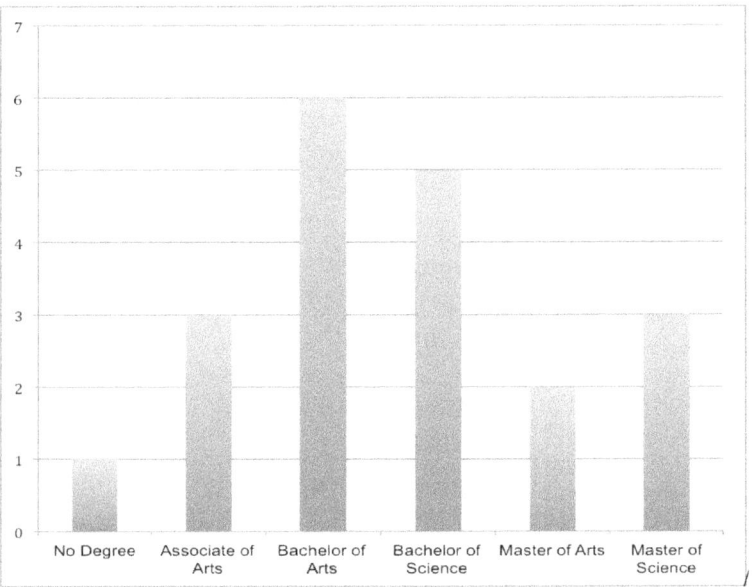

Figure 2 - Educational Distribution of Participants

An interesting data point emerged from demographic interview question number six, "Will you be eligible to retire within the next 5 to 10 years?" Participants were informed this question was optional, should anyone decide not to answer. All participants elected to answer, as depicted in Figure 4 below.

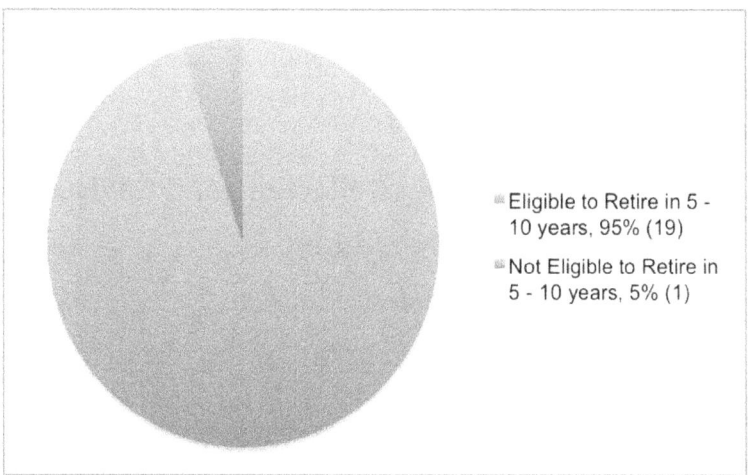

Figure 3 - Participants Eligible to Retire in the Next 5 to 10 Years

This data point will be explored in the data
analysis section as it pertains to organizational
readiness when 19 of the 20 research participant's
will be eligible to retire in the next 5 to 10 years, along
with the recommended implementation of a robust
knowledge management program in the Government
Security organization. Prior to beginning the data
collection phase, the researcher attended an online
ATLAS.ti 7 Qualitative Data Analysis Workbench
training session on February 18, 2014, hosted by
Ricardo B. Contreras, PhD, Director ATLAS.ti
Americas Training and Partnership Development. The
training session was instrumental toward

understanding the nuances of the qualitative data analysis software.

Instrumentation, Data Collection, and Analysis Procedures

Participants were solicited by the researcher to participate in the study using a solicitation script (see Appendix B). Participants who chose not to participate were to contact the researcher through company electronic mail. All purposefully selected participants elected to the part of the study. The researcher provided a letter of introduction (see Appendix A) and informed consent form (see Appendix C) to individuals who elected to be part of the study. When the researcher received the signed informed consent form from each of the 20 participants, the interviews took place. The face-to-face and telephone interviews took place over two months, from November 20, 2013 through January 30, 2014. The researcher conducted the telephone and face-to-face interviews at various conference rooms located within the aerospace facilities. There were seven face-to-face interviews and 13 telephone interviews to accommodate employees located outside of California.

Prior to beginning the face-to-face and telephone interviews, the researcher instructed the participants there were six demographic questions and nine content related questions. The participants were advised the interviews would be digitally tape recorded as stipulated on the informed consent form. The researcher reminded each participant of the one-hour interview time constraint on the participant's personal time. The researcher reiterated to each participant participation in the study would remain anonymous and each participant could voluntarily terminate his or her participation in the study at any time without consequence. Prior to initiating the interview, the researcher asked each research participant if they had questions or required clarification. The researcher observed few questions pertaining to the 15 main interview questions. The participants did not have to answer demographic question number 6: "Will you be eligible to retire within the next 5 to 10 years?" However, all participants agreed to answer demographic question number six.

During the telephone and face-to-face interviews, the researcher observed participants personally relating to the knowledge-sharing concept and showed a genuine interest to the potential effect to the security organization upon the retirement of Baby Boomers. One interesting phenomenon occurred: 19 of the 20 participants would be eligible to retire in the next 5 to 10 years. The researcher specifically noted this fact, since all of the participants were aware of the effect of lost knowledge within the government security organization. For example, participant S7 stated, "I am definitely interested in the topic," and stated further, "the reason why I really wanted to do this is that I have a very diverse set of programs and the transition between requirements is very difficult." The face-to-face and telephone interviews consisted of 15 open-ended semi-structured questions, with six demographic questions, and nine content questions specific to the four research questions.

Data Analysis.

The interpretive phenomenological method of inquiry provided participants lived experiences and perceptions of the qualitative study. Participants shared their individual lived experiences regarding

knowledge sharing in an industrial security

organization. The descriptions generated from the 20

transcribed interview responses were analyzed and

interpreted to satisfy the phenomenological criteria.

Emerging central themes, descriptions, and

characteristics were identified and recorded from the

individual experiences of the research participants.

Data analysis included categorizing the data, coding

the data into families, and compiling relevant data that

would describe the lived experiences of each

research participant. The ATLAS.ti 7 data analysis

software program was instrumental in organizing the

interviews in a primary document, similar to a

container, and allowing the researcher to analyze the

data, quotations, codes, linkages, and memos. The

primary document by research participant's

transcribed interviews consisted of approximately 127

pages for all 20 compiled interviews. A modified van

Kaam methodology was used to analyze the interview

responses. After bracketing the researcher's

experiences, an analysis of data occurred by reducing

the information to significant statements then

combining the statements into themes (Creswell,

2012). A textural description of *what* the participants experienced is documented; to include a structural description of *how* participants experienced the phenomenon to include textural and structural descriptions of the phenomenon under study was conducted (Moustakas, 1994).

Modified van Kaam Method of Analysis of Phenomenological Data.

The modified van Kaam methodology used to analyze the phenomenological data consisted of eight steps in the analysis of each transcribed interview (Moustakas, 1994). The van Kaam method of analysis comprised eight steps and was applied to the study as indicated below (Moustakas, 1994).

Step 1: Listing and preliminary grouping. Step 1 of the van Kaam methodology consisted of statements of how participants experienced the phenomenon. The researcher systematically listened to each digitally recorded interview, and read and reviewed each of the 20 manually transcribed interviews. The qualitative data analysis software program ATLAS.ti 7 provided organization and tracking of the data. The project file used to carry out analysis is identified as the Hermeneutic Unit (HU) as the container used to hold everything needed to interpret the data (Friese, 2012). The primary document contained the 20 verbatim, transcribed interviews, where the creation of quotations and coding occurred. The interpretation of data into codes and themes requires the researcher to assign categories, develop themes, build descriptions, and assign labels to the codes (Creswell, 2012).

Approximately 65 invariant constituents and 146 quotations generated from the 20 verbatim, transcribed interviews. However, the extracted information contained repetitive statements, some responses that overlap, and vague responses. The next step involved identification of invariant constituents of the experience. The researcher reduced the verbatim interview transcripts through the elimination of redundant and unnecessary statements. Each transcript was prepared, coded, sorted, and structured to discover patterns, themes, processes, and sequences using the qualitative data analysis software, ATLAS.ti 7. Furthermore, a spreadsheet database was used to organize and restructure 65 invariant constituents and 146 quotations into descriptive and abstract codes. The researcher merged the 65 invariant constituents into six core themes after three rounds of recoding and restructuring. The data analysis process took approximately two weeks to complete.

Step 2: Reduction and elimination. This step tested participant expressions for two conditions: (a) Do the expressions contain an experience essential for understanding it? and (b) Can the expression be abstracted and labeled? If so, the expression is a horizon of experience (Moustakas, 1994). The expressions were removed if they did not meet the standard described above. Overlapping, recurring, and unclear expressions were removed or offered in more exact and expressive language. The remaining prospects were invariant constituents of the occurrence. This step required the researcher to review each transcript to ensure it described the participants lived experiences and perceptions of the phenomenon. The nine content related interview questions solicited specific responses to the four main research questions. A contextual evaluation consisted of the researcher listening to digitally recorded verbatim interviews after conducting and reviewing each transcript from the participants to ensure responses corresponded with the four main research questions. Each transcript underwent a review prior to condensing the material. The transcript review consisted of identifying participants' lived experiences and perceptions toward knowledge sharing in a government security organization and organizational readiness when Baby Boomers retire. Upon completion of the review process, the researcher evaluated the feasibility of abstracting and labeling each expression to ensure robust data collection. All data codes were labeled and abstracted to ensure a more conceptual structure to the list. Any vague expressions that did not describe participant lived experiences and insights of the phenomenon were removed (Moustakas, 1994). The remaining descriptions of lived experiences and responses remained as invariant constituents (Moustakas, 1994).

The researcher clustered and labeled each of the transcribed interviews as core themes of the experience. This process consisted of two phases; phase 1 required the researcher to use the qualitative data analysis software, ATLAS.ti 7, to identify themes from the verbatim, transcribed interviews. All interviews were clustered into one primary document and uploaded to the ATLAS.ti 7database. The researcher reviewed, labeled, and categorized each expression for future analysis. The researcher assigned a coded label to each participant's experience and perception obtained from the face-to-face and telephone interviews. The coding structure consisted of the researcher classifying each expression to capture meaning and essence in the data. Each expression or participant quotation was coded with the appropriate label. The codes are short texts used to classify a large number of textural units (Friese, 2012). Once the researcher applied codes to the transcribed data, phase two consisted of the identification of core themes as invariant constituents. ATLAS.ti 7 was instrumental in creating Microsoft Excel version 2010 reports (e.g., code list, code hierarchy, quotation references, and code neighbors). Phase two consisted of theming, labeling, and reducing 65 invariant constituents into six core themes. The clustered and labeled constituents represented the six core themes emerging from participant experiences. The software database spreadsheet helped to organize and structure responses to invariant constituents. The invariant constituents displayed by number of participants who experienced the phenomenon and by the percentage of participants who experienced this phenomenon.

Step 3: Clustering and theming. Step 3 of the van Kaam method of analysis required the researcher to cluster invariant constituent's experiences into thematic labels, with the remaining constituents emerging as core themes of participant experiences. Step 3 involved the comprehensive identification of the invariant constituents and themes that described the experiences and insights of the participants conducted through three rounds of sorting, ordering, and structuring of data codes using the qualitative data analysis software program ATLAS.ti 7. Duplicate data codes with similar labels were merged into one code list for final identification of the six core themes. This process entailed listening to each digital recording, and reviewing each verbatim transcript to validate and record any missed experience or perception that may not were captured during the initial review of the digitally recorded interviews, and transcribed interviews. Significant patterns emerged from the clustering of each participant's individual experiences and perceptions. There were six clustered and labeled invariant constituents that emerged from the clustering and theming process. The following list of six core themes were identified and noted below:

1. Knowledge sharing in an industrial security organization
2. Obstacles to knowledge sharing in an industrial security organization
3. Mentoring in an industrial security organization
4. Generational differences toward knowledge sharing in an industrial security organization
5. Knowledge gaps in an industrial security organization
6. Strategic implications of knowledge sharing in an industrial security organization.

Core Theme 1: Knowledge sharing in an industrial security organization. Both security managers and industrial security specialists provided similar responses regarding their lived experiences and perceptions of sharing knowledge with less experienced employees. The following eight invariant constituents emerged for industrial security managers: applying risk management, Baby Boomer experience, collaborating, formal mentoring program, managers motivating teams, open communication, sharing experiences, tacit/tribal knowledge. In contrast, the following six invariant constituents emerged for industrial security specialists: desktop instructions, journaling, on-the-job training, relationship building, influence, and management support. Essentially the following invariant constituents emerged as core themes: effective knowledge sharing in an industrial security organization by managers and by industrial security specialists. Analysis revealed nine participant managers, or 90% of the participants, experienced this phenomenon, while 10 or 100% of the industrial security specialist's participants provided lived experiences and perceptions toward sharing knowledge with less experienced personnel. The sharing of knowledge with less experienced personnel was very important to security professionals, citing the need to develop individuals who would be replacing departing Baby Boomers in the next 5 to 10 years. This intermediate gap of employees with 6 to 10 years of work experience is an inherent risk to the security organization and included in this research study.

Core Theme 2: Obstacles to knowledge sharing in an industrial security organization. The emergence of the following seven invariant constituents from the data analysis provided significant observations from the participants: business complexities, changes in company and government, lack of formal mentoring program, lack of formal succession planning, leaving employees in the same position for several years, lack of sharing by less senior personnel, and organizational structure conducive to sharing. The lived experiences of security professionals provided insight into their perceptions of obstacles to sharing knowledge. Analysis revealed obstacles to sharing knowledge in an industrial security organization emerging as a core theme in this study. Four (20%) of security personnel provided lived experiences of relationship building, and 13 (65%) of the security specialists provided their lived experiences of mentoring Generation X and Y employees as obstacles to sharing knowledge as sub-themes in this study. The lived experiences and perceptions of security personnel indicated the importance of building and sustaining relationships with customers, and business partners gleaned from their experience as industrial security leads or managers supporting government programs. Industrial security personnel provided their lived experience and perceptions about their methodology for mentoring Generation X and Y employees as a significant part of their duties and responsibilities.

Core Theme 3: Mentoring in an industrial security organization. The emergence of the following six invariant constituents was observed from the data analysis: the need to build future leaders, sharing knowledge and experience, empowerment, cross-training, coaching and counseling, and motivating employees. Formal and informal mentoring invariant constituents emerged as sub-themes, with

mentoring in an industrial security organization
emerging as a core theme. Ten (50%) of security
personnel provided their lived experiences toward the
importance of mentoring security personnel.
Delegating to less experienced personnel was
identified as an invariant constituent among industrial
security personnel. Ten individuals (50%) of industrial
security personnel delegated duties to less
experienced personnel. Security professionals
exhibited enthusiastic responses from their
experience with mentoring less experienced
personnel by imparting knowledge and experience
from years of experience as security professionals.
The observations from these interviews provided
incentives to stimulate older knowledge workers to
share knowledge is essential to this study.

**Core Theme 4: Generational differences
toward knowledge sharing in an industrial
security organization.** The following four invariant
constituents were identified by the researcher: do not
want to repeat history, younger generation not ready
to take over, need for challenging assignments, and
the older generation not sharing knowledge and

experience. The invariant constituent, generational differences toward knowledge sharing in an industrial security organization emerged as a core theme in the study. The emergence of the sub-themes of the younger generation challenged with backfilling Baby Boomers. With 12 (60%) industrial security personnel providing their lived experience, and older, less senior security personnel unwilling to share knowledge comprised of four (20%) industrial security personnel providing their lived experience and perceptions about this invariant constituent. Industrial security professionals provided candid experiences regarding generational differences between Baby Boomers and Generation X and Y employees. The inherent differences were in regard to how work is performed, job knowledge, motivation, attention to detail, and having a sense of urgency as some of the acknowledged issues confronting security professionals.

Core Theme 5: Knowledge Gaps in an industrial security organization. The following four invariant constituents were identified: (a) experience gap of intermediate employees, (b) delegating to less

experienced personnel, (c) sustainment of processes
and procedures, and (d) unified sharing. Knowledge
gaps in an industrial security organization emerged as
a core theme of this study. The following two sub-
themes emerged from interviewing individuals about
their lived experiences and perceptions in an
industrial security organization: (a) the need for
addressing an intermediate gap of qualified security
personnel when Baby Boomers retire, with 15 (75%)
of the security personnel providing their lived
experiences and perceptions of this theme. Six (30%)
of the industrial security individuals provided their
individual experiences and perceptions toward the
sustainment of processes and procedures as sub-
themes. Security personnel provided open and honest
assessments of the potential experience gap between
new and older employees, if senior leaders fail to
address knowledge gaps in the next five years.
Security professionals acknowledged the gap
between younger employees and Baby Boomer
employees or employees with the company with 6 to
10 years of service. Security personnel provided lived
experience and perceptions about the criticality of
identifying recent college graduates with an interest in

government security as a career option.

Core Theme 6: Strategic implications of knowledge sharing in an industrial security organization. The following significant invariant constituents emerged and were observed: (a) increasing international business, (b) formal decision-making process, (c) certification courses, (d) knowledge sharing as a strategy, (e) formal development program, (f) formal leadership program for first line leaders, (g) understanding government regulations, (h) integration within the business, and (i) workforce dynamic. The strategic implications of knowledge sharing in an industrial security organization emerged as a core theme in this study. The following invariant constituents emerged as sub-themes, knowledge-sharing strategies with 12 (60%) of industrial security professionals providing their lived experiences and perceptions. Twenty (100%) of the industrial security professionals provided their lived experience and perceptions of having an infrastructure in place to support a knowledge management program. Industrial security personnel were in agreement with exercising a knowledge sharing strategy with their personnel, albeit not formalized, and were cognizant of their role and expectation to implement a knowledge sharing strategy. All 20 (100%) of the security professionals interviewed acknowledged they experienced an infrastructure that supported knowledge sharing among security personnel.

Step 4: Finalizing and validation. Step 4 of the van Kaam method of analysis required the researcher to validate invariant constituents and themes generated from the 20 verbatim, transcribed interviews: (a) Are the themes clearly articulated in the transcript? (b) Are the themes similar if not clearly articulated?, and (c) If the themes are not clear or similar, then they should be removed (Moustakas, 1994). This process required the critical review of invariant constituents by core themes with each participant's transcribed interview and digitally recorded interview. Each participant response was evaluated using the qualitative data analysis software program ATLAS.ti 7 to validate the accuracy of participants lived experience and perceptions regarding the potential loss of knowledge and organizational readiness when Baby Boomers begin to retire from the security organization.

Step 5: Construction of an individual textural description. Step 5 of the van Kaam methodology consisted of validating invariant constituents and themes by creating individual textural descriptions of the encounters and insights of the participants (Moustakas, 1994). The participants were managers and non-managers, with responses containing management biases in certain circumstances. Verbatim examples represented what participants experienced regarding the potential loss of knowledge and organizational readiness when Baby Boomers began to retire from the security organization.

Textural descriptions of participants.

Research participant M1 described his experience and perception regarding the potential loss of knowledge in the industrial security organization when Baby Boomers retire. The participant stated, "if you don't have processes and procedures established, you don't have people trained to them, or then someone leaves you don't have foundational understanding of what the person did then how can you bring that next person in." The comment, while important and shared by 50% of the participants, stressed the importance of having established and sustained processes and procedures in place prior to Baby Boomer departures. All participants observed the transformation of having immature process and procedures to an organization with roust mature processes.

Additionally, research participant M1 was adamant that knowledge transfer was only one piece of the step, "it's about knowing what to do and how to do it." Having an understanding of this concept is critical to the sustainment of the systems that were put in place. Research participant M1 did not see knowledge transfer as a potential problem for the organization. The participant's concern was the ability to motivate employees to perform and sustain the processes and procedures that were put in place to avoid security violations that could cause irreparable harm to the company.

Research participant M2 shared a personal experience regarding how the participant reaches out to peers for support. The method was contrary to the other participants because of the nature of the security business, where information is controlled and parsed out to individuals with a need to know (what is going on). Research participant M2 stated, "Anyway, I felt very comfortable going to other security professionals and say talk with me, mentor me, help me out a little bit, share with me some of your experiences, give me some of your thoughts." However, an interesting observation by research participant M3 revealed a lack of formal knowledge sharing in the industrial security organization. According to research participant M3, "There is no formal knowledge sharing, its all word of mouth, tribal knowledge … throwing people into the frying pan … that kind of thing." This statement was not reflective of the other 19 participants feelings. In fact, only research participant M3 candidly shared feelings about the lack of senior management support with providing a qualified backup to sustain a new business unit, when Baby Boomers began to depart. During the interview with research participant M3, the participant was profoundly upset about the lack of senior management support providing a qualified backup in high visibility areas of the organization. The role of mentoring in the industrial security organization emerged as a theme during the face-to-face and telephone interviews. While a formal mentoring program was not in place, it was a topic of concern for all industrial security practitioners. Research participant M4 provided the following statement,

I believe in setting up with all the personnel that work for me; that one day I will be working for them, and they can't get there without me sharing the knowledge and experience and taking on more of a mentorship type role with my personnel.

This participant was the only individual of the 20 participants who expressed a passion for empowering the team to share knowledge. This statement revealed a lived experience of empowering industrial security team members by delegating tasks to less experienced personnel with the underlying assumption they will be challenged with the ability to compete for positions with increased responsibilities.

Research participant M4 went on to confirm their convictions by stating the following, "they are empowered to make those decisions based upon two conditions that they communicate and coordinate and that will include me too," which is reflective of participant M4's willingness as a manager to allow team members to make critical decisions on their own. However, research participant M4 indicated first level managers are not provided training when assuming their positions. With limited training, first-line managers accept their roles and usually rely on experienced managers for assistance, should they need support. Research participant M4 seemed to become agitated when describing the lack of senior leadership support when individuals announced their retirement, and the lack of opportunity to simultaneously train a replacement before they arrive at the work location. The conversation focused back to the original question to help calm the participant's emotions.

Research participant S1 shared lived experiences and perceptions about their experience supporting a key business strategy for the aerospace company in the international arena. One observation revealed the need to have a qualified backup replace research participant S1, given the high visibility and importance of the position in which the participant worked. For example, while research participant S1 was on medical leave the organization did not have a qualified backup in place to step in and conduct business. This was a lesson learned since research participant S1 was the only individual possessing signature authority as the facility security officer (FSO). According to research participant S1, the position performed a key role in providing security services overseas to help business partners work through contractual requirements essential to obtaining future Department of Defense contract work. The participant's knowledge and experience identified them as a knowledge expert who will require a qualified and competent backup to take the participant's place in the organization if, and when, the participant retires from the security organization in the next 5 to 10 years. As research participant S1 stated, "I am constantly learning and sharing information." This statement is reflective of their role as the subject matter expert in the field over the last

30 years in the industrial security organization.

Research participant S2 represented an individual who possesses key knowledge in a new business arena. The participant informed the researcher of their willingness and eagerness to provide their input into the knowledge transfer research. This statement reflected a concern if a qualified replacement is not found, "I can honestly tell you that there are only one or two managers in our entire organization that understand, even close to this area." This statement was indicative of the lack of awareness of the complexity of research participant S2's responsibilities, especially when the participant will retire in the next five years. As the subject matter expert in the participant's field, this position is important to new business activities at the aerospace company. The participant's comment reflected the complexity and importance of having a qualified individual who can step in to support a critical and significant part of the business base for the aerospace company.

All 20 participants expressed their concern about not having enough time and resources to effectively mentor their employees. Participant S5

candidly expressed a concern regarding senior
security personnel not taking on mentorship roles.
Research participant S5 stated,

> But, I think we are lacking, with a lot of the
> senior guys like myself, taking roles of
> mentorship, kind of showing them the insights
> of dealing with the customers; especially some
> of the customers we have that are kind of
> difficult.

Participants were emphatic and eager to
mentor, but the daily business commitment intervened
with their goal and objective of mentoring younger
employees. Participants addressed the emerging
issue of younger inexperienced personnel who will not
be in a position to take over as Baby Boomers retire if
knowledge transfer opportunities do not occur.
Research participant S7 introduced the customer
perspective regarding their willingness to accept
contractor changes. The participant identified the
government customer's displeasure when "things
change" or when things do change an incremental
change the customer can live with. However,
research participant S7 did voice displeasure with the

reluctance to bring in a replacement when managers know an employee is leaving the organization. Bringing in a replacement before an employee retires, offers managers the ability to mentor, train, and transfer knowledge without having to lose months of rework and the inability to use a new hire awaiting access to begin work. As research participant S7 stated,

> Currently, the practice is to wait until that individual departs before bringing in someone to backfill that position, requiring a restart, which usually increases costs and you end up reworking and starting from the beginning on a project or task.

The aerospace company industrial security organization is far reaching, stretching across the country and the globe. Offsite locations not part of the shared service group (SSG) are at a disadvantage because of the inability to obtain security resources readily available to security organizations part of the shared services organization. Research participant S8 supported an offsite location in Hawaii, but could not obtain important information or resources essential to delivering security services to the customers. Another theme that emerged from research participant S10 was the lack of younger employees coming into the industrial security organization.

The following statement by research participant S10 resonated with the researcher, "The problem is that young people don't come into security, so everybody you get is 40 years old out of the military or someplace else, you just don't have young people coming in." This phenomenon revealed the difficulty of replacing qualified Baby Boomer subject matter experts who will retire from the industrial security organization in the next 5 to 10 years. With the impending Baby Boomer retirements and the need to fill the gap of intermediate employees, this is a topic of great concern for industrial security leaders.

Step 6: Construction of individual structural description. Step six of the van Kaam methodology required the researcher to create individual structural descriptions of research participant experiences based on the individual textural description and creative differences (Moustakas, 1994). The creative differences of each research participant explained the participants lived experience and perceptions of loss of knowledge and organizational readiness when Baby Boomers retire. Step six of the van Kaam methodology required the researcher to create a structural description of how they experienced the phenomenon in terms of the conditions, situations, or context (Creswell, 2012).

Structural description for research participant M1. Research participant M1 was a long-term aerospace employee and the architect of many of the organization's common processes and procedures essential for employee development and professionalism among industrial security professionals. Coincidentally, the participant would retire from the aerospace company within the next few months after the research study was conducted, taking volumes of tacit and explicit knowledge out of the workforce. The participant's breadth of knowledge and experience helped create processes and procedures that could improve organizational effectiveness and efficiencies. Participant M1 identified the organizational structure as an obstacle to sharing among industrial security personnel. Advocating the facilitation of the organizational structure, and if anyone would care to impart or share something they think is important, as the main impediment to knowledge sharing in the industrial security organization.

Structural description for research participant M2. Research participant M2 described the use of electronic communication as problematic when communicating with his personnel. The lack of individuals having face-to-face meetings was diminishing. According to the participant, there is no substitute for one-on-one communication, citing generational differences with younger employees opting to use electronic communication over face-to-face interaction. He found it much more effective to walk around the corner to have a face-to-face discussion with a colleague. The generational differences would be an underlying theme throughout the research as an obstacle to sharing knowledge, both from younger employees to older employees and vice versa.

Structural description for research participant M3. Research participant M3 is another long-term employee in the industrial security organization. The participant's knowledge and experience helped to address knowledge sharing impediments of the lack of time to share knowledge. The participant would acknowledge over-worked personnel as well as over-staffed managers as obstacles to sharing knowledge. Participant M3 cited a sphere of influence of seven or eight employees as another obstacle to sharing knowledge with staff members and constant interruptions when the exchange did occur. Additionally, the participant indicated individuals just logging their time to retire as impediments to sharing knowledge. Participant M3 suggested implementation of a job rotation program to integrate younger personnel into the special programs arena.

Structural description for research participant M4. Research participant M4 explained that time was the biggest impediment to knowledge sharing among teammates. The issue of not having enough time to share or enough time to receive information was obstacles cited by M4. Participant M4 discussed the importance of delegating tasks to the lowest level to ensure knowledge transfers throughout the organization. The empowerment of individuals was a common theme throughout the research. Industrial security managers who were comfortable and confident in their positions were more inclined to share knowledge.

Structural description for research participant M5. Research participant M5 described the system as an obstacle to sharing knowledge. For example, the compartmentalization of certain jobs is as an obstacle to sharing knowledge. The participant cited the inability to get people accessed into a special program as a virtual impossibility within nine months. However, the lack of job security was a reason for older employees not sharing knowledge. The unwillingness to share knowledge is a leadership challenge. Leaders face the challenge of incentivizing Baby Boomer employees to share knowledge. Additionally, leaders must break down the fear of sharing knowledge to understand that the more knowledge you give away, the more important you are. This would be a common theme among the participants.

Structural description for research participant M6. Research participant M6 described the participant's lived experience and perceptions regarding the obstacles to sharing knowledge among security personnel. The participant was a long-term industrial security manager supporting a regional security office. Participant M6 cited some people feel knowledge sharing is giving up power. Mentoring the wrong person could be problematic leading to the passing on of poor practices. Managers need to be involved with who is leading or mentoring individuals to ensure it is done correctly; the individuals who are not following or don't believe in the process can be detrimental to the organization.

Structural description for research participant M7. Research participant M7 described their lived experiences and perceptions regarding the obstacles to sharing knowledge in an industrial security organization. Knowledge sharing barriers came in the form of personality conflicts and resistance to change. The need to rely on the integrated product teams (IPT) to remove the barriers is important to moving forward with knowledge sharing initiatives. An interesting point was discussed regarding a new management incentive plan that relies on rewarding productive managers from a forced distribution process. According to participant M7, this process could be counterproductive to managers wanting to share their knowledge knowing the incentive is to distinguish themselves from other managers.

Structural description for research participant M8. Research participant M8 described their lived experiences and perceptions regarding the obstacles to knowledge sharing in their organization. Participant M8 is located in the eastern region of the country and described a different perspective about barriers to knowledge sharing. Participant M8 did not see any obstacles to sharing knowledge, but after further discussion revealed the need to have trustworthy employees. Participant M8 wanted employees to know what they know, realizing there are personnel issues that remain confidential. The participant does not have any personnel who are ready to retire in the next 5 to 10 years, nor anyone they do not trust, and hopes people trust him.

Structural description for research participant M9. Research participant M9 is a regional security manager responsible for providing security support to many programs and intelligence efforts. Participant M9 described the need to have a formal process to share knowledge with industrial security personnel. Participant M9 cited the pressure of time as an obstacle because knowledge sharing is not a primary responsibility. Participant M9 suggested making knowledge sharing part of every manager's roles, accountability, and authority (RAA); this would formalize and improve employee engagement in knowledge sharing activities.

Structural description for research participant M10. Research participant M10, who is responsible for an offsite location, described their lived experiences and perceptions regarding obstacles to knowledge sharing. According to the participant, the biggest obstacle to knowledge sharing is time and availability of the personnel, making it difficult to have everyone on the same page. The participant was able to train backup in all security disciplines after learning of organizational changes. This study provided lived experiences and perceptions from managers and industrial security specialists, or team lead level 5 personnel. The following descriptions and experiences involved industrial security specialists.

Structural description for research participant S1. Research participant S1 had primary responsibility for international security at the United States-based aerospace company, tasked with providing security support to new business. The participant described lived experiences and perceptions regarding the challenges faced in sharing knowledge as a one-person operation. As a one-person operation, the participant is tasked with interfacing with various security personnel across the enterprise and overseas. The participant performs a critical function that requires security expertise of how to operate internationally. Not being part of a team is an obstacle making it difficult to transfer knowledge.

Structural description for research participant S2. Research participant S2 provides essential security support to new business activities. The candid discussion of the participant lived experiences and perceptions about the obstacles to sharing knowledge was a subject of great interest. The participant's unique position requires an understanding of all security disciplines. Participant S2 was adamant about the younger generation's willingness to accept change, opposed to older employees who were set in their ways, which is a critical component of knowledge sharing.

Structural description for research participant S3. Research participant S3 described their lived experiences and perceptions of the obstacles to knowledge sharing in the industrial security organization by placing responsibility on managers for providing their support. Long-term personnel used the security organization as a stepping-stone into other careers.

Structural description for research participant S4. Research participant S4 described their lived experiences and perceptions about having a willingness to share knowledge. Participant S4 mentioned the prevailing thought for sharing knowledge in the security organization that says, "if I share, I am going to lose my competitive advantage in security." The participant's personnel would not fall victim to not sharing knowledge, opting to have them know as much as he knows. The obstacles to sharing knowledge in this scenario rest with the team leader modeling a sharing environment. As a long-term industrial security specialist, the participant is aware of the job's role and responsibly for implementing a knowledge sharing atmosphere. The participant will be retiring in 5 to 10 years, making knowledge sharing a department initiative.

Structural description for research participant S5. Research participant S5 described their lived experiences and perceptions regarding time and workload as obstacles to knowledge sharing. This common theme developed from the interviews with industrial security managers and specialists. Participant S5 found themself doing all the work to save time, which is contrary to cross-training initiatives. Participant S5 acknowledged the problems of falling into the trap of doing the work because of the specialized knowledge and the time it would take to train an inexperienced security specialists. This was a topic for further discussion in this study.

Structural description for research participant S6. The lived experiences and perceptions of participant S6 revealed no obstacles to sharing knowledge. Participant S6 described personality traits of security personnel that could make it difficult to share information. Participant S6 mentioned that the staff over which they have oversight consisted of a couple of individuals in their 30s and most of the team is in their 50s, making the managed staff a, more mature in age, industrial security team.

Structural description for research participant S7. Research participant S7 provided their lived experiences and perceptions of the obstacles to knowledge sharing. As a long-term employee with over 25 years in the industrial security field, the participant was familiar with the challenges

of motivating younger and older industrial security
personnel. Today's challenges are different from
when the participant first began their career. For
example, employees today expect promotions without
fully understanding security processes and
procedures. Participant S7 brought up a repeated
issue of leaving employees in positions for a
significant amount of time. This was another emerging
theme requiring management attention. Some
managers do not take the time to know and
understand their employees, choosing to leave them
in a position without finding out if they have the
needed skill set.

*Structural description for research
participant S8.* Research participant S8 discussed
the lack of time and money as obstacles to sharing
knowledge. Employee focus is on the work at hand to
address the need to transfer knowledge, which will
only exacerbate the problem of not participating in
knowledge sharing activities. An additional obstacle
was the geographical location of a facility if one
supports an offsite location. Resources are difficult to
obtain, which compounds the participant's ability to

adequately provide training. The recurring theme of not having enough time and money to conduct effective knowledge sharing can be an issue requiring leadership involvement.

Structural description for research participant S9. Research participant S9 provided their lived experiences and perceptions illustrating the difficulties of sharing knowledge if someone does not understand security processes and procedures. Another obstacle is the organizational structure itself, where staffs are not large enough to perform knowledge sharing or on-the-job training, and the geographic location of security offices not having adequate resources. According to participant S9, the hardest thing to accomplish is cross-training. The cross-training activity is an important activity toward sharing knowledge. However, from an organizational perspective, increasing the budget to accommodate additional staff could be a consideration by security leadership.

Structural description for research participant S10. Research participant S10 provided their lived experiences and perceptions about the obstacles to knowledge sharing. One aspect that emerged was the observation of having security personnel trained on all security disciplines versus the prevailing thought of training security personnel as specialist. If personnel do not have training on security disciplines, it makes it difficult to move any individual to other positions in which he or she may not have received training.

Step 7: Construction of Textural-Structural Description. Step 7 of the van Kaam methodology involved the researcher creating textural and structural descriptions of the meanings and essences of research participant experiences, which included incorporation of the invariant constituents, themes, and patterns (Moustakas, 1994). The compilation of participant lived experiences and insights of the phenomenon follows.

Core Theme 1: Knowledge sharing in an industrial security organization. Both industrial security managers and industrial security specialists expressed their methods of sharing knowledge with their staff. All 20 participants provided their methods of knowledge sharing, but expressed concern with the problem of not having enough time or resources to formally share knowledge with their teams. The sharing of tacit or tribal knowledge was another area of concern for managers and security specialists. Both groups expressed valid concerns about the need to share that information residing in their heads. All security managers and specialists were participating in knowledge sharing with industrial security personnel through process action teams (PAT), integrated product teams (IPT), on the job training (OJT), and desktop instructions (DI).

Core Theme 2: Obstacles to knowledge sharing in an industrial security organization.

Industrial security managers and industrial security specialists expressed concern that a formal mentoring program with emphasis on younger generation employees is nonexistent in the industrial security organization. However, four participants described the need to build relationships with customers and business partners as a potential obstacle to sharing knowledge. Industrial security managers and security specialists were providing informal mentoring to their younger personnel. This occurred through staff meetings, manager communications down to teams, and one-on-one meetings with staff.

Core Theme 3: Mentoring in an industrial security organization. Industrial security managers and industrial security specialists shared their lived experiences and perceptions regarding mentoring. Each participant participated in mentoring activities with less experienced personnel. This was not a formal process. Participants found themselves engaged with their team through open and honest communication, and transparency with each employee. While time and resources is an obstacle to sharing knowledge, mentoring is a viable option that would be vital to incorporate it as a formal and/or informal management process in the company attention. All participants observed the importance of mentoring younger employees, but a lack of time and resources prevented detailed mentoring of their team members. Mentoring consisted of hands-on experience of performing a security function.

Core Theme 4: Generational differences toward knowledge sharing in an industrial security organization. Industrial security managers and industrial security specialists identified generational differences affecting the ability to share knowledge. The inherent problem of backfilling departing Baby Boomers could be an impediment to sharing knowledge with less experienced personnel. The younger generation employees have a different method of acquiring and sharing knowledge. Less senior employees face the challenge of sharing their knowledge since they have expressed reluctance in learning the security industry through established curriculum and training. Older generation employees have exhibited a reluctance to share knowledge for fear of losing their job and not understanding the benefits of sharing knowledge. Participants expressed a desire to have mentoring added to their performance management plan to ensure it becomes a strategic imperative. Participants were delegating down tasks to less experienced personnel ensuring they would know what their manager or team lead knows.

*Core Theme 5: Knowledge gaps in an industrial security organizatio*n. The industrial security managers and industrial security specialists identified the gap in intermediate employees when Baby Boomers retire from the security organization. Once Baby Boomers begin to retire, experienced employees with 10 to 15 years of service departments are in jeopardy of losing knowledge. Currently, there are younger generation employees, individuals with 0 to 8 years' experience and older generation employees with 20 years or more experience. A gap of intermediate employees with 6 to 10 years of experience is occurring in the security organization was identified at the time of this research. Some participants were aware of the phenomenon, and were taking steps to hire younger personnel, while trying to avoid the standardized hiring of ex-military and ex-police personnel.

Core Theme 6: Strategic implications of knowledge sharing in an industrial security organization. The industrial security managers and industrial security specialists provided insight into the strategic implications of knowledge sharing. All participants described having knowledge

management as a strategic imperative. The inclusion

of a knowledge sharing initiative expressed as a

recommendation from each research participant.

Knowledge management was important to the

engineering community, but promulgation to the

industrial security organization was not occurring.

Step 8: Composite Description of the

Meanings and Essence. Step 8 of the van Kaam

methodology included the creation of a composite

description of the connotation and real meaning of the

experience from the individual textural-structural

descriptions (Moustakas, 1994). The researcher

described the results of the interpretive

phenomenological study to acquire a deeper

understanding of the individual experiences and

perceptions of 20 industrial security professionals

representing a United States-based aerospace

company. In this Chapter, the researcher interviewed

20 industrial security professionals to ascertain their

lived experiences and perceptions regarding

organizational readiness and the potential loss of

knowledge when Baby Boomers retire from the

industrial security organization. The researcher interviewed 10 Baby Boomer industrial security managers and 10 industrial security specialists face-to-face and by telephone to obtain the essence of knowledge sharing in an industrial security organization. The van Kaam method of data analysis in steps 1 through 3 consisted of grouping significant statements, followed by determining the invariant constituents through reduction and elimination, and clustering and constructing themes invariant constituents of researcher experience. The creation of textural and structural descriptions from the invariant constituents and themes for each of the participant took place. The final van Kaam process consisted of the development of a composite description that included the meaning and essences of each research participant (Moustakas, 1994).

The researcher identified six core themes in this study. All but one of the participants acknowledged the importance of knowledge sharing and identified examples of how they conducted knowledge sharing within their organizations. However, 65% of the participants explained that mentoring Generation X and Y personnel could be an obstacle to knowledge sharing, citing time, and resources as impediments to sharing knowledge. All 20 participants addressed the need for a formal mentoring program to help share knowledge across boundaries. Each research participant understood the need to develop less experienced personnel, but understood the financial burdens that prevented this from occurring. Interestingly, 75% of the participants acknowledged the knowledge gaps that could occur when subject matter experts retire from the organization. Sixty percent of the participants described the generational differences between Baby Boomers and Generation X and Y personnel as potential obstacles to sharing knowledge. Older employees with less seniority were observed as retaining their knowledge and citing job security and knowledge as power as reasons not to share knowledge.

Data Saturation and Outliers.

The researcher achieved data saturation by conducting three rounds of coding in the identification of themes and patterns. The remaining codes and themes produced six core themes that described the lived experiences and perceptions of the participants. Researcher observed outliers that acted differently than the rest of the population (Shank, 2006). Furthermore, management training emerged as an outlier as an opportunity to prepare first level managers for senior level positions. This outlier was extreme in comparison to identified core themes that focused on Generation X and Y personnel. Another outlier that emerged from the interviews focused on leaving lower level employees in their positions more than five years without offering increased responsibility or addressing development opportunities. Older security personnel who lacked motivation to share knowledge emerged as an outlier in this study. This phenomenon is critical to implementing and sustaining an effective knowledge management program in the industrial security organization. Finally, the ex-syndrome emerged as an outlier in the hiring of ex-military, police, and intelligence agency new hires opposed to internal talent and reaching out to local college recruits in an effort to diversify the security organization.

Summary

The principal aim for conducting this interpretive phenomenological research study was to understand the individual experiences and perceptions of Baby Boomer industrial security managers and industrial security specialists regarding organizational readiness and loss of knowledge when Baby Boomers retire. The researcher interviewed 10 industrial security managers and 10 industrial security specialists. The face-to-face and telephone interviews resulted in the emerging of six core themes that described the lived experiences of each participant. The use of ATLAS.ti7 assisted in compiling and organizing significant data elements central to this study. The qualitative data analysis software program reduced manual tasks and increased the legitimacy of the research results. The use of the Van Kamm method for data analysis provided a systematic approach toward answering the research questions from a personal perspective. A majority of the research participants expressed life experiences from security knowledge obtained from having over 15 years of experience in the industrial security organization.

Core Theme 1 described knowledge sharing activities performed by each research participant. This theme was central to understanding if knowledge sharing was occurring in the industrial security organization by managers and industrial security specialists.

Core Theme 2 was significant to the study as each participant described the obstacles to sharing knowledge with the impending Baby Boomer retirements. Participants expressed the need to mentor and prepare Generation X and Y employees as a critical component to sustaining the security organization in the next 5 to 10 years. Core Theme 3 described mentoring and delegating tasks to less experienced personnel as necessary to moving the organization forward while Baby Boomers are still onsite. This theme was central to implementing knowledge transfer methods prior to Baby Boomer retirements.

Core Theme 4 identified the generational differences toward knowledge sharing as a critical component in preparing the younger generation

(Generation X & Y) employees for assuming additional responsibilities toward career development. The added problem of older personnel unwilling to share their industrial security knowledge with younger employees could leave the organization without subject matter experts. Participants addressed the need for knowledge management to become a strategic initiative in order for employees to take it seriously.

Core Theme 5 presented potential knowledge gaps of younger employees as potential impediments toward preparing for Baby Boomer retirements. Participants acknowledged the gap of intermediate personnel, individuals with 6 to 10 years of experience, who may not be qualified to take over once Baby Boomers retire.

Core Theme 6 presented the strategic implications of knowledge sharing in the industrial security organization. Participants expressed the urgency to create a knowledge management program to ensure sustainment of the industrial security organization. Each research participant identified the organizational infrastructure as a necessary component to supporting a knowledge management initiative. The construction of textural-structural descriptions provided an integrated synthesis of meaning of participant experiences. This was the last step in the Van Kamm methodology that captured the universal essence of knowledge sharing in the industrial security organization. Each participant expressed the need for a structured knowledge sharing approach, but emphasized the lack of time and resources required to share knowledge across boundaries. Data saturation revealed commonality among research participants through interview questions designed to promote discussion of knowledge sharing activities occurring in the industrial security organization. Research participants reviewed their interview responses for accuracy before the researcher transcribed each interview. The repetitive nature of the interview responses toward organizational readiness when Baby Boomers retire provided anticipatory responses by the researcher, which contributed to data saturation.

The lack of employees who were motivated to share knowledge emerged as an outlier in this study. Lack of diversification in the industrial security organization was another outlier that emerged from this study. Once viewed as a male dominated career, industrial security is now enticing to women as careers. Another outlier that emerged in this study was the emphasis on building relationships with customers. This aspect was identified as a lost art among new security practitioners who may not understand the need to cultivate and maintain a relationship with customers and business partners.

Chapter 5 provides conclusions, implications, and recommendations from the data collection and analysis conducted in Chapter 4. Chapter 5 offers an overview of the six core themes identified from the researcher's data collection and analysis. Additionally, Chapter 5 contains knowledge management implementation strategies for security leaders, and the recommendation to include further research in the area of knowledge transfer in an industrial security organization.

CHAPTER V

SUMMARY, CONCLUSIONS, AND

RECOMMENDATIONS

The purpose for conducting this interpretive
phenomenological study was to explore the individual
experiences and perceptions of aerospace company
industrial security managers and industrial security
specialists and the potential loss of knowledge and
organizational readiness when Baby Boomers retire.
The study included 10 industrial security managers
and 10 industrial security specialist's level 5
employees representing a United States-based
aerospace company with an office in the Northwest,
Southwest, Midwest, and Eastern regions of the
country. Chapters 1 and 2 examined the Baby
Boomer knowledge-sharing phenomenon and
provided a comprehensive literature review to support
knowledge sharing in an industrial security
organization. The discussion in Chapter 3 regarded
the rationale for selecting the van Kaam research

methodology for the phenomenological study. Chapter 4 revealed the data collection, analysis, findings, and summary of the research study. The study emphasized the importance of corporations in creating, capturing, sharing, and transferring essential knowledge to the remaining Generation X and Y employees once Baby Boomers retire from the security organization.

Chapter 5 concludes with a thorough discussion of the six core themes that emerged from the data collection and analysis that occurred in Chapter 4. Chapter 5 includes the interpretation of the research findings, implications of the study, significance to security leaders, and recommendations for additional research.

The Review of the Research Study.

The study originated in response to the potential loss of knowledge occurring in companies across the United States when Baby Boomers retire and the ability to retain and use that knowledge. Additionally, the widening skills gap among older and younger security personnel emerged as a central theme in preparation for Baby Boomer retirements. The potential loss of knowledge could be detrimental to the United States-based aerospace company's competitive advantage. While extensive literature reviews encompassed knowledge management as a topic, there was an opportunity to add to existing literature regarding experiences and perceptions of aerospace industrial security workers and loss of knowledge when Baby Boomers retire. A gap in the literature existed because no research into the lived experiences and perceptions of security personnel has occurred in an industrial security environment. The threats of lost knowledge and gap in skills are central to Baby Boomer retirements (DeLong, 2004). While literature reviews on knowledge transfer was prevalent in other manufacturing organizations, industrial security knowledge worker studies did not occur. The economic collapse occurring during the years of 2007- 2009 provided leaders an opportunity to create knowledge transfer plans before Baby Boomers retired (Ball & Gotsill, 2011).

Employing an interpretive phenomenological research method, in conjunction with the van Kaam method of analysis, the researcher examined the lived

experiences and perceptions of 10 industrial security
managers and 10 industrial security specialists level 5
personnel as they provided essence of the meanings
of their experiences with knowledge sharing in an
industrial security organization. Research questions
created by the researcher, and designed for
examination of participant experiences and insights
regarding the loss of knowledge and organizational
readiness when Baby Boomers retire from the
industrial security organization.

The phenomenological study included the
following four research questions:

RQ1: What are the lived experiences of
industrial security managers transferring?

RQ2: What are the lived experiences of
industrial security specialists transferring knowledge
from more senior employees to newer employees?

RQ3: What lived experiences prevent sharing
industrial security knowledge at the aerospace
company?

RQ4: What knowledge management strategies are used to ensure industrial security knowledge transfers from retiring senior employees to newer employees?

Chapter 3 of the interpretive phenomenological study described the research methods used to conduct the study and gather the data. A phenomenological study employing van Kaam's method of analysis was suitable for this study because it provided awareness to an impending problem of lost knowledge and organizational readiness when Baby Boomers retire. The van Kaam method of analysis for use in the collection, organization, and analysis phase of the research study proved advantageous to the researcher. Research participant experiences and perceptions were essential to understanding organizational readiness in sustainment and improving the organizations competitive advantage in the next 5 to 10 years. The phenomenological interview explored and gathered experiential material used for reflection to help provide a rich individual experience (Van Manen, 2014). The researcher conducted a pilot study with three industrial security professionals each with more than 15 years of security experience and as managers. All three pilot study participants were interviewed in-person to refine the interview questions prior to dissemination to the 20 main study participants (Creswell, 2012).

The van Kaam method of analysis introduced common patterns and core themes from the analysis and review of the invariant constituents regarding lost knowledge and organizational readiness when Baby Boomers retire. The six core themes that emerged from the analysis correlated to the research participant responses to the 15 semi-structured interview questions.

Core Theme 1: Knowledge sharing in an industrial security organization

Core Theme 2: Obstacles to knowledge sharing knowledge in an industrial security organization

Core Theme 3: Mentoring in an industrial security organization

Core Theme 4: Generational differences toward knowledge sharing

Core Theme 5: Knowledge Gaps in an industrial security organization

Core Theme 6: Strategic implications of knowledge sharing in an industrial security organization

Examining each research participants lived experiences and perceptions provided an opportunity to understand the essence of the meanings security professionals placed on knowledge sharing and organizational readiness when baby boomers leave the company.

Conclusions and Interpretations

Findings for Core Theme 1: Knowledge Sharing in an Industrial Security Organization.

With the exception of one research participant, the majority experienced and participated in knowledge sharing activities with their respective team members. Research participants acknowledged the importance of sharing knowledge with less experienced personnel as the primary objective. However, the realization of Baby Boomer retirements without having experienced personnel to take over weighed heavily on participants' minds. An understanding of knowledge transfer is essential to effective knowledge sharing (Ghobadi & D'Ambra, 2012). However, participants expressed discontent with not having enough time or resources to conduct effective knowledge sharing activities. This response could be elevated to senior leaders to ensure first line managers and team leads can allocate time for effective knowledge sharing in the security organization. Incentive opportunities for Baby Boomer employees should be addressed by senior leaders to ensure knowledge sharing occurs, before retirements.

Findings for Core Theme 2: Obstacles to Knowledge Sharing Knowledge in an Industrial Security Organization.

Participants indicated that failing to mentor Generation X and Y personnel, prior to Baby Boomer departures from the aerospace company, was as a primary obstacle to knowledge sharing. Participants indicated relationship building was an obstacle to sharing knowledge. The participants acknowledged the need to establish trust as a prerequisite to effective knowledge sharing. A lack of trust building exercises and basic infrastructure proved to be obstacles to effective knowledge sharing activities in the industrial security organizations (Paulin & Winroth, 2013). With the emergence of several invariant constituents, the common theme of an unwillingness to share knowledge by older security personnel became a constant from Baby Boomer managers and security specialists.

Findings for Core Theme 3: Mentoring in an Industrial Security Organization.

Effective mentoring of less experienced industrial security personnel was a reoccurring theme among the participants. All participants expressed the need to build future leaders by creating mentoring programs to facilitate knowledge sharing. The participants relied upon informal mentoring practices to ensure their less experienced personnel receive developmental opportunity in their respective departments. Siegel and Schultz (2011) suggested formal mentoring programs could lead to management and leadership development opportunities. The importance of ensuring security personnel collaborate with knowledgeable mentors was a central theme. Additional comparison and evaluation of the benefits of formal versus informal mentoring is a topic for future discussion with senior security leaders to understand better the best approach toward mentoring less experienced security personnel.

Findings for Core Theme 4: Generational Differences toward Knowledge Sharing in an Industrial Security Organization.

Effective knowledge sharing in the security organization cannot occur if leaders fail to address the gap of intermediate employees left behind when Baby Boomers depart the industrial security organization in 5 to 10 years. The sustainment of processes and procedures is central to the security organizations competitive advantage over similar aerospace companies. Each research participant provided experiences of having younger and older personnel on their teams, short of intermediate experienced personnel who will replace retiring Baby Boomers. Participants cited a potential lack of collaboration between Baby Boomers, Generation X, and Y personnel as generational knowledge sharing barriers. Another interesting emergent theme was the willingness of senior security members to share knowledge with less experienced personnel. Further detailed discussions revealed a lack of time and resources as inhibitors to knowledge sharing among Baby Boomers and Generation X and Y cohorts.

Mchenry and Ash (2013) discussed the silo mentality
as an organizational barrier to cross-functional
sharing. The silo mentality is another phenomenon
that requires further review, because of its prevalence
in the special programs arena by virtue of
compartmentalization of information.

**Findings for Core Theme 5: Knowledge Gaps in
an Industrial Security Organization.**

Study participants expressed their lived
experiences and perceptions regarding the gap in
knowledge that would occur once subject matter
expert Baby Boomers retired from the security
organization. Knowledge gaps occurring in the
industrial security organization could be significantly
affected if qualified security personnel fail to be
trained prior to Baby Boomer retirements. An
emphasis on experience versus age was a predictor
for identifying subject matter experts to address
knowledge gaps in the security organization (Dunham
& Burt, 2011). The empowerment of less experienced
personnel provided an opportunity to close the gap
between experienced and inexperienced industrial

security personnel. Empowerment of workers creates a sense of meaning, competence, and self-determination toward sharing their knowledge (Dunham & Burt, 2011). Individuals who possess key industrial security knowledge can facilitate knowledge transfer within the security organization. The identification and cultivation of knowledge subject matter experts are critical to knowledge sharing in an industrial security organization.

Findings for Core Theme 6: Strategic Implications of Knowledge Sharing in an Industrial Security Organization.

The strategic implications of knowledge sharing in a United States-based aerospace company are instrumental for sustaining a competitive advantage. Senior security leaders face challenges of creating and implementing a knowledge management program that will address the 52% of Baby Boomer retirements expected to occur within the next 5 to 10 years. The identification of qualified and competent replacement personnel will be daunting. The constant company and customer changes will force security personnel to acquire relationship-building skills to compete with other aerospace industrial security organizations. Organizational knowledge is a strategic resource itself, as recent data confirms that 50% of NASAs workforce is eligible to retire (Ramanigopal, 2012). This is a significant problem since the Baby Boomer retirement phenomenon is not just a United States workforce issue, but also a global concern. With recent government budget reductions, United States-based aerospace companies are challenged with being cost-effective and more productive (Ramanigopal, 2012). All participants expressed concern about having a robust infrastructure in place to accommodate an effective knowledge management program.

In contrast, knowledge sharing among industrial security professionals is dependent upon management engagement by including knowledge transfer as a performance management objective. Industrial security personnel who are eligible to retire in the next 5 to 10 years are concerned with not having adequate resources or time to perform knowledge transfer within their departments. Industrial security personnel acknowledge budgetary and management involvement as key areas of concern to effective knowledge transfer.

Progressive management styles lead to effective knowledge transfer initiatives in certain regions of the country. This is an opportunity to model to the rest of the enterprise in contrast to the research participant's views that most organizations were not inclined to share knowledge. The majority of the industrial security organizations have older employees; choosing to retire could potentially jeopardize national security.

The research study indicates participants believed this type of plan would reduce effective knowledge transfer as result of their lived experiences and the interviews. One emerging theory was the role women managers played in the male dominated career field of industrial security. Management theorists suggested the belief that women are more emotional than men are resulting in a void of women placed in senior level positions (Yuki, 2010). Continued research in the area of women in management is critical to fostering equality in the workplace. A future study in the area of women leaders in the security and fire protection industry could lead to better understanding and improved leadership theory in an aerospace arena.

Implications of the Study to Leadership.

The implications of this interpretive phenomenological study to leadership is a responsibility for identifying development opportunities for less experienced personnel. While leaders tend to concentrate on high performing employees, individuals who have great potential remain a key resource for the organization. Leaders are responsible for developing employees, but at times fail because of self-interest of climbing the corporate ladder, which correlates to distrust among personnel. Leaders are responsible for working with declining budgets, limited resources, and implementation of reward systems for sharing knowledge (Ramanigopal, 2012). The impending Baby Boomer exodus will adversely affect corporations around the country and globally. The implications to leaders will directly influence how leaders and managers motivate Generation X and Y employees in the future by providing a challenging work environment and opportunities for advancement. Leaders were accustomed to employees staying with their companies for 20 and 30 years, but that has changed; employees are not motivated to stay for long periods, desiring more challenging assignments, as well as instant rewards and gratification. Leaders are at a crossroads regarding how they will influence remaining employees who may not have a similar work ethic, education, and company loyalty as do Baby Boomers.

The traditional leadership focus was on transformational and charismatic leaders, where the leader has the power over their followers through a command and control style of leadership (LaRue, Childs, & Larson, 2004). The change in corporate America with youthful workers will cause leaders to re-evaluate how they manage the technically adept and provide a challenging work environment for Generation X and Y employees. The leadership change will see the hierarchical pyramid turned upside down. The CEO and senior management will act in a support role allowing individuals to function in a leadership role (Andert, 2011). This leadership paradigm change could eliminate the power and leadership phenomenon that dominates the traditional leader-follower management style. This potential change could be advantageous to employers if the change leads to improved productivity and performance of Generation X and Y employees.

Limitation of Research

A shortcoming of this interpretive phenomenological research study was confining the study to the industrial security organization of 550 employees while omitting commercial aircraft security and site security organizations. Another limitation was the lack of comparison between male and female industrial security managers participating in knowledge creation and sharing activities. With an emphasis on diversity, the unique United States-based aerospace company involved in this research study is promoting and including females in key leadership positions. Restricting the research to the private sector could have limited the study's effectiveness. Expanding the study to the public sector could lead to productivity and efficiencies of organizations of similar size and scope. The omission of senior security and fire protection leaders supporting international activities could yield important insight into knowledge creation and sharing perspectives in the defense and commercial aircraft divisions. The inclusion of technical subject matter experts in the security and fire protection organization could yield discussion of the technical challenges toward knowledge sharing in the security organization.

Significance of Research

The significance of the interpretive phenomenological study was providing awareness to an impending problem of the potential loss of knowledge and organizational readiness when Baby Boomers retire. At the time of this study, 54% of the security and fire protection Baby Boomer personnel are eligible to retire in the next 5 to 10 years. However, drawing attention to this phenomenon might encourage organizational leaders to create knowledge management programs to assist personnel with knowledge sharing initiatives. The research provided lived experiences and perceptions from subject matter experts, industrial security managers and industrial security specialists, in the industrial security organization who are poised to help ensure organizational sustainment. Senior leaders are in a position to respond to the core themes identified within this study as opportunities to develop knowledge management programs that could improve the organizations competitive advantage.

Recommendations for Implementation

As an industrial security manager located in Southern California, this researcher provided topics for consideration at an S&FP leadership offsite meeting in early April 21 and 22, 2014. The focus of the offsite meeting was impending Baby Boomer retirements, attracting, hiring, developing, and retaining talented people who will be shaping the organization into the future. The growing urgency to create and implement a knowledge management program designed to create, capture, share, and transfer knowledge from departing Baby Boomer employees to Generation X and Y employees is a strategic initiative. Recommendations for implementing knowledge transfer initiatives will rely upon management support and encouragement to ensure knowledge sharing occurs.

Additionally, senior security and fire protection leaders can leverage knowledge management experience from existing enterprise subject matter experts to effectively transition to a knowledge sharing culture. Furthermore, effective communication among senior leaders in government security, site security, and commercial aircraft security is paramount to implementing an effective knowledge transfer program in the security organization. However, leadership responsibility is critical to motivating Baby Boomers employees to share their knowledge with less experienced personnel. The inclusion of knowledge sharing as a business goal and objective on performance reviews will align with the organizational strategy providing managers with a formal process for managing knowledge sharing. Manager engagement with employees is critical to motivating employees to share knowledge from individuals who are reluctant to share what they know to less experienced personnel. Managers will have to be creative with motivating and incentivizing employees to share knowledge.

Recommendations for Future Research

With four generations co-existing in today's organizations, leaders must be able to apply diverse thought in how they communicate, motivate, and manage in this environment. Additional emphasis is on the knowledge gap of intermediate employees, creation of a formal mentoring program, older employees unwilling to share knowledge, and motivating younger generation employees to join the security and fire protection organization. The research study findings reinforced current knowledge management literature. Organizations that are not prepared for Baby Boomer retirements face challenges of sustaining a competitive advantage. However, a major finding of organizations not having skilled personnel to take the place of departing Baby Boomers becomes a strategic imperative for the United States-based aerospace company. Ball and Gotsill (2011) posited that manufacturing organizations are not drawing people to replace mature workers. Manufacturing, which encompasses aerospace, food processing, metalworking, and automotive industries face challenges of finding newly trained and skilled personnel to step in for retired Baby Boomers (Ball & Gotsill, 2011). This phenomenon is not restricted to the United States, but has global implications. The industrial security organization is a complex business unit that is essential to national security. Research in the area of industrial security has not occurred, which makes this study unique in the findings and recommendations to security leaders. In addition, the lack of a robust knowledge management program identifies opportunity to field teams to pursue strategies for identifying, collecting, sharing, and storing key knowledge.

A reluctance to share knowledge from older employee to younger employees is another finding addressed in current literature. Delong (2004) posited that differences between Baby Boomers and Generation X employees will undermine motivation for knowledge sharing and learning in organizations. Security and fire protection leaders face challenges of creating and cascading knowledge management strategies down to line employees to ensure sustainment and competitive advantage. However, complications with sharing knowledge across DoD and special program boundaries challenge leaders and managers to be innovative and creative in deploying effective knowledge management initiatives. Furthermore, future research should focus upon all levels of leadership in the S&FP organization to better understand how widespread the problem of Baby Boomer retirements and the effect on the organization. Future studies should include an examination of female managers and female level 5 personnel across the enterprise to ascertain if gender contributes to knowledge sharing and organizational readiness when Baby Boomers retire. The inclusion of executive level S&FP leaders would provide a leadership perspective on the potential knowledge loss and organizational readiness when Baby Boomers retire. These additional topics of research would represent all employment levels bolstering the study findings and leadership awareness.

Summary

The Baby Boomer exodus is becoming a reality in all organizations. The improvement of the economy influenced employee decisions to retire, which is effecting corporations across the United States and globally. The diverse nature of the workplace with four cohorts co-existing in the workplace will prove challenging for leaders and managers. Leaders and managers face challenges with hiring, retaining, motivating, and managing a diverse workforce in the years ahead. Furthermore, leaders face challenges of with not having skilled personnel in the pipeline to take over for departed Baby Boomers (Ball & Gotsill, 2011). These challenges are not new to leaders and managers; knowledge management initiatives were the topic of conversation among leaders and managers for some time. However, the aging of America's workforce cannot go unnoticed without taking steps to retain tacit knowledge from knowledge workers who have consistently had answers to problems that plagued the industry. The advancement in technology and science contributed to professionals and managers working in knowledge-intensive and interdisciplinary environments (DeLong 2004).

Summary of Major Conclusions.

The emergence of six core themes from the 20 semi-structured face-to-face and telephone interviews provided significant examples of opportunities to improve the competitive advantage of the United States-based aerospace company's security and fire protection organization. The six core themes that emerged were knowledge sharing in an industrial security organization; obstacles to knowledge sharing in an industrial security organization; mentoring in an industrial security organization; generational differences toward knowledge sharing in an industrial security organization; knowledge gaps in an industrial security organization; and strategic implications of knowledge sharing in an industrial security organization. The researcher concluded that senior leadership support is critical to implementing an effective knowledge management program within the security organization. The core themes provide an

opportunity for leaders to address the knowledge
sharing gaps prior to implementing an effective
knowledge management program. However, security
leaders exhibiting creativity and a willingness to
engage their employees in knowledge sharing
activities can lead to improving the competitive
advantage of the security organization.

The impetus for conducting this interpretive
phenomenological study was to examine the potential
loss of knowledge and organizational readiness when
Baby Boomers retire from the security organization.
This research study consisted of 20 face-to-face and
telephone digitally recorded interviews with 10
industrial security managers and 10 industrial security
specialists level 5 employees. The study results
provide S&FP executive leadership with better
awareness of knowledge sharing and knowledge
transfer implications when Baby Boomers retire from
the industrial security organization. While the S&FP
leaders recently acknowledged the need to create a
knowledge management program, considerable
opportunities exist to create additional knowledge
transfer methods. The literature review revealed the
immediate need to establish knowledge sharing and

knowledge transfer methods before Baby Boomers depart, otherwise that intellectual capital walks out the door. This study addressed the need for knowledge transfer methods, such as cross-training, job rotation, job shadowing, formal mentoring, and improved succession planning. More important, the motivating of older employees to share their knowledge will be critical for sustaining a viable knowledge management program. Additionally, the topic for further consideration was the development of first line leaders for senior manager positions.

The impending departure of Baby Boomer employees is a phenomenon occurring across all industries in the United States. Therefore, this research is generalizable to large firms, both public and private, to ensure knowledge transfers from Baby Boomers to Generation X and Generation Y employees. However, small or medium firms face challenges of not having adequate staffing, financial resources, and expertise to accommodate retiring employees and potential loss of knowledge (Durst & Wilhelm, 2012).

More important, a firm's financial position affects the ability to train and develop individuals to take over for retiring personnel in small or medium sized firms. An awareness of the potential loss of knowledge can affect an organizations competitive advantage if preparation does not occur. Organizations with long-term experienced personnel performing complex tasks require robust knowledge management programs to ensure organizational sustainment.

The potential loss of knowledge in corporations is not limited to the United States-based aerospace company. The following industries will suffer the biggest impact manufacturing, educational services, public administration, and health services if knowledge transfer programs fail to absorb knowledge from departing Baby Boomers (Ball & Gotsill, 2011). Additionally, problems have emerged with Generation X and Y individuals choosing to forego careers in the manufacturing or blue-collar jobs, along with a lack of interest in engineering and science. More importantly, companies that do not have knowledge transfer programs in place to train less experienced Generation X and Y personnel will be in a position of not having skilled personnel ready to replace departing Baby Boomers. Furthermore, an organizations competitive advantage weakens when the remaining workforce does not possess the knowledge, skills, and abilities to sustain the organization.

REFERENCES

Aaron, B. (2009). Determining the business impact of knowledge management. *Performance Improvement*, 48(4), 35-45. Retrieved from ABI/INFORM Global. (Document ID: 1791947001).

Aerospace Industries Association (2010, May 19). Retrieved from http://www.aia-aerospace.org/

Ajith Kumar, J., & Ganesh, L. S. (2009). Research on knowledge transfer in organizations: A morphology. *Journal of Knowledge Management, 13*(4), 161-174. doi:10.1108/13673270910971905

Aktharsha, U. S. (2011). A theory of knowledge management. *Journal of Contemporary Research in Management, 6*(1), 103-119.

Allah, H. B. (2011). *The influence of multi-generational cohorts on organizational leadership: A phenomenological study.* (University of Phoenix). *ProQuest Dissertations and Theses, 173.*

Amirkhani, A., Tajmirriahi, J., Mohammadi, M., & Dalir, M. (2012). Assessing the effectiveness of knowledge management in empowering and development of human resources: A case study on Ati Luleh Sepahan Company. *Interdisciplinary Journal of Contemporary Research in Business, 3*(12), 131-147. Retrieved from http://ijcrb.webs.com/

Anantatmula, V. (2009). Designing meaningful KM processes to improve organizational learning. *Trends in Information Management, 5*(2), 219-245.

Andert, D. (2011). Alternating leadership as a proactive organizational intervention: Addressing the needs of the Baby Boomers, Generation Xers and Millennials. *Journal of Leadership, Accountability and Ethics, 8*(4), 67-83.

Arain, M., Campbell, M. J., Cooper, C. L., & Lancaster, G. A. (2010). What is a pilot or feasibility study? A review of current practice and editorial policy. *BMC Medical Research Methodology, 10*67-73. Retrieved from http://www.biomedcentral.com.ezproxy.apollolibrary.com/

Arora, E. (2011). Knowledge management in public sector. *Researchers World, 2*(1), 165-171.

Auerbach, C. F., & Sliverstein, L. B. (2003). *Qualitative Data: An Introduction to Coding and Analysis.* New York: New York University Press.

Ball, K., & Gotsill, G. (2011). *Surviving the Baby Boomer exodus: Capturing knowledge from Gen X and Y employees.* Boston, MA: Course Technology.

Barachini, F. (2009). Cultural and social issues for knowledge sharing. *Journal of Knowledge Management, 13*(1), 98-110. doi:10.1108/13673270910931198

Bass, B. M. (1990). *Bass and Stogdill's handbook of leadership: Theory, research, and managerial applications* (3rd ed.). New York, NY: The Free Press.

Becerra-Fernandez, I., Gonzalez, A., & Sabherwal, R. (2004). *Knowledge management: Challenges, solutions, and technologies.* Upper Saddle River, NJ: Prentice Hall. Retrieved from The University of Phoenix eBook Collection.

Bergin, M. (2011). NVivo 8 and consistency in data analysis: reflecting on the use of a qualitative data analysis program. *Nurse Researcher, 18*(3), 6-12.

Berliant, M., & Fujita, M. (2009). Dynamics of knowledge creation and transfer: The two person case. *International Journal of Economic Theory, 5*(2), 155-179. doi:10.1111/j.1742-7363.2009.00104.x

Blau, P. M. (1964). *Exchange & Power in Social Life*. New Brunswick, NJ: Transaction Publishers.

Bloor, M., & Wood, F. (Eds.). (2006). *Keywords in qualitative methods*. Thousand Oaks, CA: SAGE Publications Ltd. doi: 10.4135/9781849209403

Blum, P. (2010). Michael Polanyi: The anthropology of intellectual history. *Studies In East European Thought, 62*(2), 197-216. doi:10.1007/s11212-010-9110-2

Bratianu, C., & Orzea, I. (2010). Tacit knowledge sharing in organizational knowledge dynamics. *Proceedings of the European Conference on Intellectual Capital*, 107-114. Retrieved from http://academic-conferences.org

Buckley, S., & Giannakopoulos, A. (2011). *Sharing knowledge - the CoP way*. Paper presented at the 72-VII.

Caldwell, R. (2012). Leadership and Learning: A Critical Reexamination of Senge's Learning Organization. *Systemic Practice & Action Research, 25*(1), 39-55. doi:10.1007/s11213-011-9201-0

Calo, T. (2008). Talent management in the era of the aging workforce: The critical role of knowledge transfer. *Public Personnel Management, 37*(4), 403-416.

Cane, S., McCarthy, R., & Halawi, L. (2010). Ready for battle? A phenomenological study of military simulation systems. *The Journal of Computer Information Systems, 50*(3), 33-40.

Carmeli, A., Atwater, L., & Levi, A. (2011). How leadership enhances employees' knowledge sharing: The intervening roles of relational and organizational identification. *Journal of Technology Transfer, 36*(3), 257-274. doi:http://dx.doi.org.ezproxy.apollolibrary.com/10.1007/s10961-010-9154-y

Creswell, J. W. (2002). *Educational research: Planning, Conducting, and Evaluating Quantitative and Qualitative Research* (2nd ed.). Retrieved from The University of Phoenix eBook Collection.

Creswell, J. W. (2008). *Educational Research: Planning, Conducting, and Evaluating Quantitative and Qualitative Research* (3rd ed.). Retrieved from The University of Phoenix eBook Collection.

Creswell, J. W. (2012). *Qualitative inquiry and research design: Choosing among five approaches* (3rd ed.). Thousand Oaks, CA: Sage Publications, Inc.

Cyr, S., & Chun, W. C. (2010). The individual and social dynamics of knowledge sharing: An exploratory study. *Journal of Documentation, 66*(6), 824-846. doi:10.1108/00220411011087832

Dalkir, K. (2011). *Knowledge Management in Theory and Practice* (2nd ed.). Cambridge, Massachusetts: The MIT Press.

DeLong, D. W. (2004). *Lost Knowledge: Confronting the threat of an aging workforce*. New York, NY: Oxford University Press, Inc.

Dinur, A. (2011). Tacit knowledge taxonomy and transfer: Case-Based research. *Journal of Behavioral & Applied Management, 12*(3), 246-281.

Draghici, M., & Petcu, A. (2011). Knowledge Transfer - The key to drive innovation for service organizations excellence. *Journal of Knowledge Management, Economics & Information Technology, 1*(4), 44-53.

Draper, A. A., & Swift, J. A. (2011). Qualitative research in nutrition and dietetics: Data collection issues. *Journal of Human Nutrition & Dietetics, 24*(1), 3-12.

doi:10.1111/j.1365-277X.2010.01117.x

Drucker, P. F. (1999, Winter). Knowledge-worker productivity: The biggest challenge. *California Management Review, 41*(2), 79.

Duma, S., Khanyile, T., & Daniels, F. (2009). Managing ethical issues in sexual violence research using a pilot study. *Curationis, 32*(1), 52-58.

Dunham, A. H., & Christopher D. B. Burt. (2011). Organizational memory and empowerment. *Journal of Knowledge Management, 15*(5), 851-868. doi:http://dx.doi.org/10.1108/13673271111174366

Durkin, D. (2010). Managing generational diversity. *Baseline*, (105), 14.

Durst, S., & Wilhelm, S. (2011). Knowledge management in practice: insights into a medium-sized enterprise's exposure to knowledge loss. *Prometheus, 29*(1), 23-38. doi:10.1080/08109028.2011.565693

Durst, S., & Wilhelm, S. (2012). Knowledge management and succession planning in SMEs. *Journal of Knowledge Management, 16*(4), 637-649. doi:http://dx.doi.org/10.1108/13673271211246194

Dychtwald, K., & Baxter, D. (2007). Capitalizing on the new mature workforce. *Public Personnel Management, 36*(4), 325-334.

Emadzade, M., Mashayekhi, B., & Abdar, E. (2012). Knowledge management capabilities and organizational performance. *Interdisciplinary Journal of Contemporary Research In Business, 3*(11), 781-790.

Empson, L. (2001). Fear of exploitation and fear of contamination: Impediments to knowledge transfer in mergers between professional service firms. *Human Relations, 54*(7), 839-862.

English, M. J., & Baker, Jr., W. H. (2006). *Winning The Knowledge Transfer Race: Using your company's knowledge assets to get ahead of the competition*. New York, NY: McGraw-Hill.

Foss, N. J., Minbaeva, D. B., Pedersen, T., & Reinholt, M. (2009). Encouraging knowledge sharing among employees: How job design matters. *Human Resource Management, 48*(6), 871-893.

Franklin, L. (2009). Meno's Paradox, the slave-boy Interrogation, and the unity of Platonic recollection. *Southern Journal Of Philosophy, 47*(4), 349-377.

Friese, S. (2012). *Qualitative Data Analysis with ATLAS.ti*. Thousand Oaks, California: Sage Publications Ltd.

Gagné, M. (2009). A model of knowledge-sharing motivation. *Human Resource Management, 48*(4), 571-589.

Galagan, P. (2010, February). Bridging the skills gap: New factors compound the growing skills shortage. *T + D, 64*(2), 44-49, 6.

Ghobadi, S., & D'Ambra, J. (2012). Knowledge sharing in cross-functional teams: A coopetitive model. *Journal of Knowledge Management, 16*(2), 285-301. doi:http://dx.doi.org/10.1108/13673271211218889

Gibbs, G. R. (2002). *Qualitative data analysis: Explorations with NVivo*. Retrieved from The University of Phoenix eBook Collection.

Glorgl, A. (2009). *The descriptive phenomenological method in psychology: A modified Husserlian approach*. Pittsburgh, PA: Duquesne University Press.

Giorgi, A., & Giorgi, B. (2008). Phenomenological psychology. In C. Willig, & W. Stainton- Rogers (Eds.), *The SAGE Handbook of Qualitative Research in Psychology* (pp. 165-179). SAGE Publications Ltd. doi: 10.4135/9781848607927.n10

Given, L. M. (Ed.). (2008). *The SAGE encyclopedia of qualitative research methods*. Thousand Oaks, CA: SAGE Publications, Inc. doi: 10.4135/9781412963909

Glogowska, M., Young, P., & Lockyer, L. (2011). Propriety, process and purpose: Considerations of the use of the telephone interview method in an

educational research study. *Higher Education, 62*(1), 17-26.
doi:10.1007/s10734-010-9362-2

Goble, E., Austin, W., Larsen, D., Kreitzer, L., & Brintnell, C. S. (2012). Habits of
mind and the split-mind effect: When computer-assisted qualitative data
analysis software is used in phenomenological research. *Forum: Qualitative
Social Research, 13*(2), n/a.

Goel, A., Rana, G., & Rastogi, R. (2010). Knowledge management as a process
to develop sustainable competitive advantage. *South Asian Journal of
Management, 17*(3), 104-116.

Goulding, C. (2002). *Grounded theory: A practical guide for management,
business and market research*. Thousand Oaks, CA: Sage Publications Inc.
Retrieved from The University of Phoenix eBook Collection.

Groenewald, T. (2004). A Phenomenological Research Design Illustrated.
International Journal of Qualitative Methods, 3(1), 1-26.

Gupta, B., Joshi, S., & Agarwal, M. (2012). The effects of expected benefit and
perceived cost on employees' knowledge sharing behavior: A study of IT
employees in India. *Organizations & Markets In Emerging Economies, 3*(1),
8-19.

Gururajan, V., & Fink, D. (2010). Attitudes towards knowledge transfer in an
environment to perform. *Journal of Knowledge Management, 14*(6), 828-
840. doi:10.1108/13673271011084880

Haller-Hayon, O. (2011). Learning by sharing: Does it improve graduates'
preparation for the working world? *International Journal of Interdisciplinary
Social Sciences, 5*(9), 143-161.

Hasan Ali, A. (2011). Organizational citizenship behavior and impacts on
knowledge sharing: An empirical study. *International Business Research,
4*(3), 221-227. doi:10.5539/ibr.v4n3p221

Hesse-Biber, S. N. (2002). *Mixed methods research: Merging theory with
practice*. New York, NY: The Guilford Press. Retrieved from The University
of Phoenix eBook Collection.

Hislop, D. (2009). *Knowledge management in organizations: A critical
introduction* (2nd ed.). New York, NY: Oxford University Press.

Hislop, D. (2013). *Knowledge management in organizations: A critical
introduction* (3rd ed.). Oxford, United Kingdom: Oxford University Press.

Hislop, D. (2010). Knowledge management as an ephemeral management
fashion? *Journal of Knowledge Management, 14*(6), 779-790.
doi:10.1108/13673271011084853

Hogan, J., Dolan, P., & Donnelly, P. (2009). *Approaches to qualitative research:
Theory & Its Practical Application*. Cork, Ireland: Oak Tree Press. Retrieved
from The University of Phoenix eBook Collection.

Hokanson, C., Sosa-Fey, J., & Vinaja, R. (2011). Mitigating the loss of knowledge
resulting from the attrition of younger generation employees. *International
Journal of Business & Public Administration, 8*(2), 138-151. Retrieved from
http://www.iabpad.com/

Holbrook, A. L., Green, M. C., & Krosnick, J. A. (2003). Telephone versus face-
to-face interviewing of national probability samples with long questionnaires.
Public Opinion Quarterly, 67(1), 79-125.

Honarpour, A., Jusoh, A., & Khalil Md, N. (2012). Knowledge management, total
quality management and innovation: A new look. *Journal of Technology
Management & Innovation, 7*(3), 22-31. Retrieved from http://www.jotmi.org/

Hoon Song, J., Kolb, J. A., Hee Lee, U., & Kyoung Kim, H. (2012). Role of
transformational leadership in effective organizational knowledge creation
practices: Mediating effects of employees' work engagement. *Human*

Resource Development Quarterly, 23(1), 65-101. doi:10.1002/hrdq.21120

Hu, M., Tsung-Lin, O., Haw-Jeng, C., & Lee-Cheng, L. (2012). Effects of social exchange and trust on knowledge sharing and service innovation. *Social Behavior & Personality: An International Journal, 40*(5), 783-800.

Iancu, E., & Buta, S. (2011). Potential developments of expert systems using information about explicit and tacit knowledge. *International Journal of Research & Reviews in Applied Sciences, 9*(3), 420-426.

Irvine, A. (2011). Duration, dominance and depth in telephone and face-to-face interviews: A comparative exploration. *International Journal Of Qualitative Methods, 10*(3), 202-220. Retrieved from http://www.ualberta.ca/~iiqm/

Jamerson, C. M. (2009). *The aging workforce: A qualitative phenomenological study of mature workers' views of younger supervisors.* (University of Phoenix). *ProQuest Dissertations and Theses,* 429-n/a.

Jiun-Shiu Chen, & Lovvorn, A. S. (2011). The speed of knowledge transfer within multinational enterprises: The role of social capital. *International Journal of Commerce & Management, 21*(1), 46-62. doi:10.1108/10569211111111694

Kirkman, B., Mathieu, J., Cordery, J., Rosen, B., & Kukenberger, M. (2011). Managing a new collaborative entity in business organizations: Understanding organizational communities of practice effectiveness. *Journal of Applied Psychology, 96*(6), 1234-1245.

Kooij, D., de Lange, A., Jansen, P., & Dikkers, J. (2008). Older workers' motivation to continue to work: Five meanings of age: A conceptual review. *Journal of Managerial Psychology, 23*(4), 364-394.

Kothari, A., Bickford, J., Edwards, N., Dobbins, M., & Meyer, M. (2011). Uncovering tacit knowledge: a pilot study to broaden the concept of knowledge in knowledge translation. *BMC Health Services Research, 11*198. Retrieved from http://www.biomedcentral.com.ezproxy.apollolibrary.com/

Krishnaveni, R. R., & Sujatha, R. R. (2012). Communities of practice: An influencing factor for effective knowledge transfer in organizations. *IUP Journal Of Knowledge Management, 10*(1), 26-40. Retrieved from http://www.iupindia.in/

LaRue, B., Childs, P., & Larson, K. (2004). *Leading organizations from the inside out: Unleashing the collaborative genius of action-learning teams* (2nd ed.). New York, NY: John Wiley & Sons, Inc. Retrieved from The University of Phoenix eBook Collection.

Lawthom, R. (2011). Developing learning communities: Using communities of practice within community psychology. *International Journal of Inclusive Education, 15*(1), 153-164. doi:10.1080/13603116.2010.496212

Leighton, J. (2010). External validity. In J. Neil Salkind (Ed.), *Encyclopedia of Research Design* (pp. 467-471). Thousand Oaks, CA: SAGE Publications, Inc. doi:10.4135/9781412961288.n146

Leiter, M., Jackson, N., & Shaughnessy, K. (2009). Contrasting burnout, turnover intention, control, value congruence and knowledge sharing between Baby Boomers and Generation X. *Journal of Nursing Management, 17*(1), 100-109. Retrieved from http:// www.cinahl.com/cgi-bin/refsvc?jid=638&accno=2010138991.

Liyanage, C., Elhag, T., Ballal, T., & Li, Q. (2009). Knowledge communication and translation - a knowledge transfer model. *Journal of Knowledge Management, 13*(3), 118-131. doi:10.1108/13673270910962914

Mathew, V., & Kavitha, M. (2008). The critical knowledge transfer in an organization: approaches. *ICFAI Journal of Knowledge Management, 6*(4), 25-39. Retrieved from http://www.icfaipress.org

Mchenry, W. K., & Ash, S. R. (2013). Knowledge management and collaboration:

Generation X vs. Generation Y. *International Journal of Business and Social Science, 4*(12).

McLaughlin, G., & Stankosky, M. (2010). Knowledge has legs: Personal knowledge strategies shape the future of knowledge work and knowledge management. *On the Horizon, 18*(3), 204-212. doi:10.1108/10748121011072654

Meisel, S., & Fearon, D. (2007). Teaching a new generation: The differences are not trivial. *Organization Management Journal, 4*(3), 287-298. doi:10.1057/omj.2007.28

Meriac, J., Woehr, D., & Banister, C. (2010). Generational differences in work ethic: An examination of measurement equivalence across three cohorts. *Journal of Business & Psychology, 25*(2), 315-324. doi:10.1007/s10869-010-9164-7

Miller, S. (2009). Phased retirement keeps boomers in the workforce. *HR Magazine, 53*61. Retrieved from http://www.shrm.org/hrmagazine/

Mills, A. M., & Smith, T. A. (2011). Knowledge management and organizational performance: A decomposed view. *Journal of Knowledge Management, 15*(1), 156-171. doi:10.1108/13673271111108756

Mládková, L. (2012). Management of knowledge workers. Presented at 766-XXV.

Moore, C. G., Carter, R. E., Nietert, P. J., & Stewart, P. W. (2011). Recommendations for planning pilot studies in clinical and translational research. *CTS: Clinical & Translational Science, 4*(5), 332-337. doi:10.1111/j.1752-8062.2011.00347.x

Moser, P. K., & vander Nat, A. (2003). *Human knowledge: Classical and contemporary approaches* (3rd ed.). New York, NY: Oxford University Press. Retrieved from The University of Phoenix eBook Collection.

Moustakas, C. (1994). *Phenomenological Research Methods*. Thousand Oaks, CA: Sage Publications, Inc.

Murphy Jr., E. F., Gibson, J., & Greenwood, R. A. (2010). Analyzing generational values among managers and non-managers for sustainable organizational effectiveness. *SAM Advanced Management Journal (07497075), 75*(1), 33-55. Retrieved from http://www.samnational.org

Nahavandi, A. (2006). The art and science of leadership (4th ed.). Upper Saddle River: Pearson. Retrieved from The University of Phoenix eBook Collection.

Neuman, W. L. (2003). *Social research methods* (5th ed.). Upper Saddle River, NJ: Prentice Hall. Retrieved from The University of Phoenix eBook Collection.

Neyland, D. (2008). *Organizational ethnography*. Thousand Oaks, CA: Sage Publications Inc. Retrieved from The University of Phoenix eBook Collection.

Ngah, R., & Jusoff, K. (2009). Tacit knowledge sharing and SMEs' organizational performance. *International Journal of Economics and Finance, 1*(1), 216-220.

Nicholls, D. (2009). Qualitative research: Part three -- methods. *International Journal of Therapy & Rehabilitation, 16*(12), 638-647. Retrieved from http://www.internurse.com/

No, Y., & Walsh, J. P. (2010). The importance of foreign-born talent for US innovation. *Nature Biotechnology, 28*(3), 289-291. doi:10.1038/nbt0310-289

Nonaka, I., & Nishiguchi, T. (Eds.). (2001). *Knowledge emergence: Social, technical, and evolutionary dimensions of knowledge creation*. Oxford: Oxford University Press. Retrieved from The University of Phoenix eBook Collection.

Nonaka, I., & Takeuchi, H. (1995). The knowledge-creating company: *How*

Japanese companies create the dynamics of innovation. New York, NY:
Oxford University.

O'Dell, C., & Hubert, C. (2011). The new edge in knowledge: How knowledge
management is changing the way we do business. Hoboken, NJ: John
Wiley & Sons, Inc.

O'Neill, B. S., & Adya, M. (2007). Knowledge sharing and the psychological
contract: Managing knowledge workers across different stages of
employment. Journal of Managerial Psychology, 22(4), 411-436.

O'Sullivan, D. & Dooley, L. (2009). Applying innovation. Thousand Oaks, CA:
Sage. Okyere-Kwakye, E., & Nor, K. d. (2011). Individual factors and
knowledge sharing. American Journal of Economics & Business
Administration, 3(1), 66-72. Retrieved from http://www.scipub.org/

Older Workers: GAO-08-630T. (2008). GAO Reports, 1. Retrieved from
http://www.gao.gov/

Oliver, M. (2010). The relevance of psychosocial indicators in community
palliative care: A pilot study. Australian Journal of Advanced Nursing, 27(3),
20-30.

Pasher, E., & Ronen, T. (2011). The complete guide to knowledge management:
A strategic plan to leverage your company's intellectual capital. Hoboken,
NJ: John Wiley & Sons, Inc.

Paulienė, R. (2012). Transforming leadership styles and knowledge sharing in a
multicultural context. Business, Management & Education / Verslas, Vadyba
Ir Studijos, 10(1), 91-109. doi:10.3846/bme.2012.08

Paulin, D., & Winroth, M. (2013). Facilitators, inhibitors, and obstacles - a refined
categorization regarding barriers for knowledge transfer, sharing, and flow.
Paper presented at the 320-XV.

Peet, M. R., Walsh, K., Sober, R., & Rawak, C. S. (2010). Generative Knowledge
Interviewing: A method for knowledge transfer and talent management at
the University of Michigan. International Journal of Educational
Advancement, 10(2), 71-85. doi:10.1057/ijea.2010.10

Petkovic, M., & Miric, A. (2009). Managing organizational knowledge while
downsizing organizations. Tourism & Hospitality Management, 15(2), 257-
265.

Polanyi, M. (1962). Personal knowledge: Toward a post-critical philosophy.
Chicago, IL: University of Chicago Press.

Polanyi, M. (1966). The tacit dimension. New York, NY: Doubleday Press.

Quinn, R. P., Gutek, B. A., & Walsh, J. T. (1980). Telephone Interviewing: A
Reappraisal and a Field Experiment. Basic & Applied Social Psychology,
1(2), 127-153. Retrieved from
http://www.erlbaum.com/Journals/journals/BASP/basp.htm

Rai, R. K. (2011). Knowledge management and organizational culture: A
theoretical integrative framework. Journal of Knowledge Management,
15(5), 779-801. doi:10.1108/13673271111174320

Ramanigopal, C. S. (2012). Knowledge Management Strategies for Successful
Implementation in Aerospace Industry. International Journal of Management
Research and Reviews, 2(10), 1725-1732.

Reester Jr., K. (2008). Dynamic succession planning: Overcoming the Baby
Boomer retirement crisis. Journal of Public Works & Infrastructure, 1(1), 97-
106. Retrieved from http://www.henrystewart.com/jpwi/index.html

Reychav, I., & Weisberg, J. (2009). Good for workers, good for companies: How
knowledge sharing benefits individual employees. Knowledge & Process
Management, 16(4), 186-197. doi:10.1002/kpm.335

Saldana, J. (2009). The coding manual for qualitative researchers. Thousand

Oaks, CA: Sage Publications Inc.

Saldana, J. (2012). *The coding manual for qualitative researchers* (2nd ed.). Thousand Oaks, CA: Sage Publications Inc.

Sasser, S. (2010). Older workers and labor force participation rates. *Franklin Business & Law Journal*, (3), 1-14. Retrieved from http://www.franklinpublishing.net

Schermerhorn, J. R., Hunt, J. G., & Osborn, R. N. (2003). *Organizational Behavior* (8th ed.). New York, New York: John Wiley & Sons, Inc. Retrieved from The University of Phoenix eBook Collection.

Senge, P. M. (1990). *The fifth discipline: The art & practice of the learning organization.* New York: Doubleday/Currency.

Settoon, R., Bennett, N., & Liden, R. (1996). Social exchange in organizations: Perceived organizational support, leader -- member exchange, and employee reciprocity. *Journal of Applied Psychology, 81*(3), 219-227. doi: 10.1037/0021-9010.81.3.219

Shank, G. D. (2006). *Qualitative research: A personal skills approach* (2nd ed.) Upper Saddle River, NJ: Pearson. Retrieved from The University of Phoenix eBook Collection.

Shin-Yuan, H., Hui-Min, L., & Wen-Wen, C. (2011). Knowledge-sharing motivations affecting R&D employees' acceptance of electronic knowledge repository. *Behaviour & Information Technology, 30*(2), 213-230. doi:10.1080/0144929X.2010.545146

Siegel, P. H., Schultz, T., & Landy, S. (2011). Formal versus informal mentoring of MAS professionals. *Journal of Applied Business Research, 27*(2), 5-11.

Simon, M. K. (2006). *Dissertation and scholarly research: Recipes for success.* Dubuque, IA: Kendall/Hunt.

Simon, M. K., & Goes, J. (2012). *Dissertation and Scholarly Research Recipes for Success: 2013 Edition.* San Bernardino, CA: Create Space Independent Publishing Platform.

Simons, N. (2010). Leveraging generational work styles to meet business objectives. *Information Management Journal, 44*(1), 28-33. Retrieved from http://www.arma.org/publications/journal/journal%5Fabout.cfm

Singh, S. (2011). Leadership & organizational learning in knowledge management practices in global organizations. *Indian Journal of Industrial Relations, 47*(2), 353-365. Retrieved from http://www.srcirhr.com/

Siu Loon, H. (2006). Tacit knowledge, Nonaka and Takeuchi seci model and informal knowledge processes. *International Journal of Organization Theory & Behavior (PrAcademics Press), 9*(4), 490-502.

Soliman, F. (2011). Could one transformational leader convert the organization from knowledge based into learning organization, then into innovation? *Journal of Modern Accounting & Auditing, 7*(12), 1352-1361. Retrieved from http://www.accountant.org.cn

Srivastava, V. (2011). Why are Workers Resistant to Sharing Knowledge?. *Proceedings Of The International Conference On Intellectual Capital, Knowledge Management & Organizational Learning*, 513-520.

Stam, C. (2009). Knowledge and the ageing employee: A research agenda. *Proceedings of the European Conference on Intellectual Capital*, 435-441. Retrieved from http://academic-conferences.org

Stancu, D., & Balu, F. (2009). Building a "Learning Organization": Case study for a banking institution. *Metalurgia International, 14*(12), 174-179. Retrieved from http://www.metalurgia.ro

Stanford Encyclopedia of Philosophy. (2007, January 11). *Evolutionary Epistemology.* Retrieved from http://plato.stanford.edu/entries/epistemology-evolutionary/

Stanford Encyclopedia of Philosophy. (2008, August 16). *Pragmatism.* Retrieved from http://plato.stanford.edu/entries/pragmatism/

Stark, E. (2009). Lost in a time warp: How age stereotypes impact older Baby Boomers who still want to work. *People & Strategy, 32*(4), 58-64. Retrieved from http://www.hrps.org/

Stevens, R. (2010). Managing human capital: How to use knowledge management to transfer knowledge in today's multi-generational workforce. *International Business Research, 3*(3), 77-83. Retrieved from http://ccsenet.org/journal

Szyjka, S. (2012). Understanding research paradigms, Trends in science education research. *Problems of Education in The 21st Century, 43*110-118. Retrieved from http://www.jbse.webinfo.lt/Problem_of_Education_Volumers.htm.

Thomas, E., & Magilvy, J. (2011). Qualitative rigor or research validity in qualitative research. *Journal for Specialists in Pediatric Nursing, 16*(2), 151-155. doi:10.1111/j.1744-6155.2011.00283.x

Todorova, N. (2011). *Value of knowledge management systems: A review paper.* Paper presented at the 475-XIV. Retrieved from http://search.proquest.com/docview/1010055870?accountid=35812

Toossi, M. (2005). Labor force projections to 2014: Retiring boomers. *Monthly Labor Review, 128*(11), 25-44. Retrieved from http://stats.bls.gov/opub/mlr/mlrhome.htm

Toossi, M. (2009). Labor force projections to 2018: Older workers staying more active. *Monthly Labor Review, 132*(11), 30. Retrieved from http://stats.bls.gov/opub/mlr/mlrhome.htm

Toossi, M. (2012). Labor force projections to 2020: A more slowly growing workforce. *Monthly Labor Review, 135*(1), 43. Retrieved from http://stats.bls.gov/opub/mlr/mlrhome.htm

Trugman-Nikol, G. L. (2011). Lost knowledge-What is the cost? *Journal of Corporate Accounting & Finance (Wiley), 22*(2), 55-60. doi:10.1002/jcaf.20662

Tuan, L. (2011). Human resource management in knowledge transfer. *International Business & Management, 2*(2), 128-138. Retrieved from http://cscanada.net/

Turcan, M. (2010). *Expectancy theory as a predictor of faculty motivation to use a course management system.* (Clemson University). *ProQuest Dissertations and Theses.*

van Aalst, J. (2009). Distinguishing knowledge-sharing, knowledge-construction, and knowledge-creation discourses. *International Journal of Computer-Supported Collaborative Learning, 4*(3), 259-287. doi:10.1007/s11412-009-9069-5

Van Manen, M. (2014). *Phenomenology of Practice: Meaning-Giving Methods in Phenomenological Research and Writing.* Walnut Creek, California: Left Coast Press, Inc.

Vroom, V. H. (1964). *Work and Motivation.* San Francisco, CA: John Wiley & Sons, Inc. Wadhwa, V. (2009). A reverse brain drain. *Issues in Science & Technology, 25*(3), 45.

Watson, S., & Hewett, K. (2006). A multi-theoretical model of knowledge transfer in organizations: Determinants of knowledge contribution and knowledge Reuse. *Journal of Management Studies, 43*(2), 141-173. doi:10.1111/j.1467-6486.2006.00586.x

Willis, N. G. (2010). *Using systems theory and social exchange theory to*

*understand factors that impact retention, turnover and motivation to work in
a public child welfare agency.* (University of Houston). *ProQuest
Dissertations and Theses,*

Wilson, K., Sin, H., & Conlon, D. E. (2010). What about the leader in leader-
member exchange? The impact of resource exchanges and substitutability
on the leader. *Academy Of Management Review, 35*(3), 358-372.
doi:10.5465/AMR.2010.51141654

Wiltshier, F. (2011). Researching with NVivo. *Forum : Qualitative Social
Research, 12*(1), n/a.

Windsperger, J., & Gorovaia, N. (2010). Knowledge and trust as determinants of
the knowledge transfer strategy in networks. *Conference Proceedings:
International Conference of the Faculty of Economics Sarajevo (ICES),* 1-
21. Retrieved from http://www.efsa.unsa.ba/site/english/

Witt, U., & Zellner, C. (2009). How firm organizations adapt to secure a sustained
knowledge transfer. *Economics of Innovation & New Technology, 18*(7),
647-661. doi:10.1080/10438590802564584

Wysocki, K. C. (2009). *A phenomenological study: Leaderships perception of
organizational readiness to address the impending Baby Boomer exodus.*
(University of Phoenix). *ProQuest Dissertations and Theses.*

Yin, R. K. (2009). *Case study research: Design and methods* (4th ed.). Thousand
Oaks, CA: Sage Publishing, Inc.

Yukl, G. (2010). *Leadership in organizations* (7th ed.). Upper Saddle River, NJ:
Prentice Hall. Retrieved from The University of Phoenix eBook Collection.

APPENDICES

APPENDIX A

Letter of Introduction

Date:
Dear:

I am a student at the University of Phoenix, School for Advanced Studies, working on a Doctoral degree in Organizational Leadership. I am conducting a research study entitled: Knowledge Transfer by Industrial Security Personnel at a United States-based Aerospace Company: A Phenomenological Study.

The purpose of this phenomenological study was to explore the lived experiences and perceptions of Baby Boomer industrial security managers and industrial security specialists from the United States-based aerospace company regarding the potential loss of organizational knowledge when industrial security personnel begin to retire and to determine organizational readiness toward capturing and sharing knowledge.

Each research participant will be requested to use their personal time to participate in an in-person or telephone interview data collection phase to ensure compliance with company time charging regulations.

Please sign and return the attached Informed Consent Agreement to Michael R. Perez, mail station, H012-A207, in a company mail transmittal envelope prior to the interview if you give permission voluntarily to serve as a participant in the study described and you are 18 years old or older.

If you have questions concerning the research study, please contact me. (POC noted here)

Sincerely,

/s/ Michael R. Perez

APPENDIX B

Solicitation Script

Hello:

My name is Michael R. Perez, and I am a student at the University of Phoenix-Online, a fully accredited University, working on a Doctoral degree in Organizational Leadership. I am conducting a research study entitled: Knowledge Transfer by Industrial Security Personnel at a United States-based Aerospace Company: A Phenomenological Study. The purpose of this phenomenological study is to explore the lived experiences and perceptions of Baby Boomer industrial security managers and industrial security specialists from the United States-based aerospace company regarding the potential loss of organizational knowledge when industrial security personnel begin to retire and to determine organizational readiness toward capturing and sharing knowledge. I am soliciting your participation in a 1 hour recorded telephone or in-person interview consisting of six demographic and nine semi-structured open-ended personal interview questions. Your participation in this study is voluntary. You will be requested to use your personal time to participate in the in-person or telephone interview data collection phase to ensure compliance with company time charging regulations. If you choose not to participate or to withdraw from the study at any time, you can do so without penalty or loss of benefit to yourself. All research documentation will be destroyed immediately when a subject withdraws from the study. The researcher will delete all electronic files, and all hard copy information will be destroyed using a cross-cut shredder to prevent reconstruction. Participants who are removed from the study will not be part of the data analysis.

The results of the research study may be published, but your name and organization's name will not be used. There are no foreseeable risks to you from participating in this research. Although there may be no direct benefit to you, a possible benefit is your participation and contribution in providing insight to leaders regarding your perception of the level of organizational readiness to address the risk of knowledge loss that will occur when Baby Boomer personnel retire. The research study seeks to create new knowledge in the field of knowledge management and in the field of organizational leadership. If you choose to participate, you will receive an Introductory Letter from your company electronic mail system with an invitation to participate in a telephone or in-person interview, and an Informed Consent Agreement form will be signed and returned to me by company mail prior to the interview. If you do not want to participate in the research study, please provide a response to the researcher through the company electronic mail system. A lack of response will signify approval to participate in the study. If you have questions concerning the research study, please contact me at (xxx-xxx-xxxx/xxx@xxxx.com or xxx@xxx.com).

APPENDIX C

Informed Consent Agreement

Informed Consent: Participants 18 years of age and older

Dear   ,

My name is Michael R. Perez, and I am a student at the University of Phoenix working on a Doctor of Management degree. I am doing a research study entitled: "Knowledge Transfer by Industrial Security Personnel at a United States-based Aerospace Company: A Phenomenological Study." The purpose of this study is to observe knowledge transfer experiences among security employees.

Your participation will involve a 1-hour in-person or telephone interview. Participants will use their own time for the interview. The interview will be tape recorded and transcribed. You can decide to be a part of this study or not. You can withdraw from the study at any time without any penalty or loss of benefits. If you withdraw, or you do not want to be part of the study, please send an email to michael.r.perez2@boeing.com. All research material will be destroyed that day a subject withdraws from the study. The researcher will delete all computer files. All hardcopy data will be shredded. The researcher will use a coding pattern to protect subject names. The researcher must have permission to use personal data to select the following: (a) managers and industrial security specialists born between 1946 and 1964; (b) have a Top Secret clearance, Special Program access; (c) eligible to retire in 5 to 10 years; and (d) work in the aerospace security office. The researcher must have permission to tape record and transcribe the interviews. The results of the research study may be published. Your identity will remain private. Your name will not be made known to any outside party.

In this research, there are no likely risks to you. Although there may be no direct benefit to you, a possible benefit from your being part of this study is a deeper understanding of knowledge transfer.

If you have any questions about the research study, please call me at (xxx-xxx- xxxx/xxx@xxxx.com or xxx@xxx.com). For questions about your rights as a study participant, or any concerns or complaints, please contact the University of Phoenix Institutional Review Board via email at IRB@phoenix.edu. As a participant in this study, you should understand the following:

You may decide not to be part of this study, or

you may want to withdraw from the study. If you want to withdraw at any time, you can do so without any problems.

Your identity will be kept private.

Michael R. Perez, the researcher, has fully explained the nature of the research study and has answered all of your questions and concerns.

You must give permission for the researcher, Michael R. Perez, to record the interviews. You understand that the information from the recorded interviews may be transcribed. The researcher will use a coded pattern to protect subject's name.

Data will be kept in a locked filing cabinet. The data will be kept for three years, and then destroyed. All computer files will be deleted. All hard copy data will be shredded.

The results of this study may be published.
Participants will use their own time when interviewed.
Permission is needed to use subject's personal information.
All emails will be protected.
Only the researcher, Michael R. Perez has access to the research data.

"By signing this form, you agree that you understand the nature of the study, the possible risks to you as a participant, and how your identity will be kept confidential. When you sign this form, this means that you are 18 years old or older and that you give your permission to volunteer as a participant in the study that is described here."

(CHECK ONE)
☐ I accept the above terms.
☐ I do not accept the above terms.

_____
Signature of the Interviewee

_____
Date

_____
Signature of the researcher

_____
Date

APPENDIX D

Interview Questions

This section contains a list of six demographic and nine semi-structured, open-ended interview questions that will be administered in-person and by telephone. The telephone interview and in-person interviews will be digitally audio recorded and transcribed by the researcher. These questions revolved around a phenomenological research study to explore the perceptions and lived experiences of industrial security managers and security specialist regarding organizational readiness to address the risk of knowledge loss that will occur when security personnel retire. The results of the six demographic and nine semi-structured, open-ended interview questions will be analyzed and incorporated into Chapter 4 (Findings).

Demographic Questions

- What is your highest level of education you have completed: A) Associate of Arts/Science Degree, B) Bachelors of Arts/Science Degree, C) Master's Degree, D) Ph.D. /Doctorate.
- What specialized security training do you have? A)

Facility Security Officer (FSO), B) Contractor Special Security Officer (CSSO), C) Contractor Program Security Officer (CPSO), D) Communications Security-COMSEC, and E) Certified Information Systems Security Professional (CISSP).

- How many years or professional experience do you have working in an industrial security field? A) 0-5, B) 6-10, C) 11-15, or D) more than 15 years.
- How many years of experience do you have as an industrial security manager or Level 5 security specialist? A) 0 through 5, B) 6 through 10, C) 11 through 15, D) More than 15 years.
- Which security discipline do you support? A) National Industrial Security Program (NISP), B) Special Programs, or C) Special Access Program (SAP).
- Will you be eligible to retire within the next 5 to 10 years? A) Yes, B) No.

Interview Questions

Content Questions

- In your experience, describe knowledge sharing situations in your organization?
- In your lived experiences, how are industrial security employees motivated to share or reuse knowledge with less experienced personnel?
- In your lived experiences, what resources are

available to assist industrial security employees with sharing knowledge with less experienced personnel?

- In your experience, why is transferring tacit knowledge (non-codified processes) to less experienced personnel important to the industrial security organization?
- In your experience as a security professional, what knowledge management strategies are being used in the industrial security organization?
- In your lived experiences, what knowledge gaps could occur in your department when Baby Boomers retire from the industrial security organization?
- From your lived experiences, what are the obstacles to sharing knowledge among industrial security personnel?
- From your lived experiences, how are you providing an environment to share knowledge?
- How is the aerospace company's competitive advantage threatened if Baby Boomers retire without sharing critical industrial security knowledge with newer employees?

APPENDIX E

Copyright Permission

Figure 1 represents a multi-theoretical model viewed as a single, complex system, depicting knowledge contribution and knowledge reuse to better understand why individuals would share knowledge for the benefit of others.

Excerpts falling within the STM Guidelines for Quotation and Other Academic Uses of Excerpts from Journal Articles. You may use the following without obtaining explicit permission from the STM publishers who are signatories to these guidelines:

- a maximum of two figures (including tables) from a journal article or five figures per journal issue (unless a separate copyright holder is identified in such figure, in which event permission should be sought from that holder);
- single text extracts of less than 100 words or series of text extracts totaling less than 300 words for quotation; and
- permitted use applies in all media and in future editions.

APPENDIX F

Premises, Recruitment, and Name, PM, Use Permission - Aerospace Company Premises

XXXXXXXXXXXX
(redacted for anonymity)

Name of Facility, Organization,
Institution, or Association

Please check mark any of the following statements that you approve regarding the study and data described below.

☒ I hereby authorize Michael R. Perez, a student of University of Phoenix, who is conducting a research study titled or described as follows: Knowledge Transfer By Industrial Security Personnel At A United States-Based Aerospace Company: A Phenomenological Study, access to, and use of the non-identifiable archival data described below as follows: Enterprise Plant Security System (EPSS) for use in the aforementioned research study. In granting this permission, I understand the following (please check mark each of the following as applicable):

☒ The data will be maintained in a secure and confidential manner.

⊠ The data may be used in publication of results from this study.

⊠ This research study must have IRB approval at the University of Phoenix before access to the data identified here is provided to Michael R. Perez.

⊠ Access to and use of this data will not be transferred to any other person without my/our express written consent.

⊠ The source of the data may be identified in the publication of the results of this study.

⊠ Relevant information associated with this data will be available to the dissertation chair, dissertation committee, and school, as may be needed for educational purposes.

(redacted for anonymity)[2]   August 20, 2012
Print Name   Date

Signature
Director of Government Security

Signature
Researcher Signature / Acknowledgement

Address of Corporate Site   March 6, 2012
(redacted for anonymity)   Date Requested

Current version 032012

---

[2] *Information throughout the dissertation that has been redacted is to strive to maintain the anonymity of the aerospace company to avoid conflict of interest, and further protect the privacy and anonymity of the research study participants, as well as the privacy of the researcher (private residence, job location, etc.).*

APPENDIX G

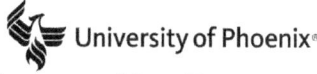 University of Phoenix®

Permission to Use Enterprise Plant Security System (EPSS) Database
(The following indicates the text and content, but is not an exact copy of the actual document sent)

University of Phoenix
Data Access and Use Permission
XXXXXXXXXXXX
(Company name redacted for anonymity)

Name of Facility, Organization, University, Institution, or Association

Please check mark any of the following statements that you approve regarding the study and data described below:

☒ I hereby authorize <u>Michael R. Perez,</u> a student of University of Phoenix who is conducting a research study titled or described as follows: Knowledge Transfer By Industrial Security Personnel At A United States-Based Aerospace Company: A Phenomenological Study, access to, and use of the non-identifiable archival data described below as follows: Enterprise Plant Security System (EPSS) for use in the aforementioned research study. In granting this permission, I understand the following (please check mark each of the following as applicable):

☒ The data will be maintained in a secure and confidential manner.

☒ The data may be used in the publication of results from the study.

☒ This research study must have IRB approval at the University of Phoenix before access to the data identified here is provide to Michael R. Perez.

☒ Access to and use of the data will not be transferred to any other person without my/our express written consent.

☒ The source of the data may be identified in the publication of the results of the study.

☒ Relevant information associated with this data will be available to the dissertation chair, dissertation committee, and school as may be needed for educational purposes.

(Redacted for anonymity)
Printed Name of Representative
Signature of Representative
Job Title of Representative
Address of Representative

Current version 03021012

August 30, 2012
Date
Michael R. Perez
Researcher Signature/Acknowledgement
March 6, 2013
Date

APPENDIX H

 University of Phoenix®

Knowledge Transfer By Industrial Security Personnel at a United States-Based Aerospace Company: A Phenomenological Study

Confidentiality Statement

As a researcher working on the above research study at the University of Phoenix, I must maintain the confidentiality of all information concerning all research participants as required by law. Only the University of Phoenix Institutional Review Board may have access to this information. "Confidential Information" of participants includes, but is not limited to: name, characteristics, or other identifying information, questionnaire scores, ratings, incidental comments, other information accrued either directly or indirectly through contact with any participant, and/or any other information that by its nature would be considered confidential. In order to maintain the confidentiality of this information, I

hereby agree to refrain from discussing or disclosing

any Confidential Information regarding research

participants, to any individual who is not part of the

above research study or in need of the information for

the expressed purposes on the research program.

This includes having a conversation regarding the

research project or its participants in a place where

such discussion might be overheard or discussing any

Confidential Information in a way that would allow an

unauthorized person to associate (either correctly or

incorrectly) an identity with such information. I further

agree to store research records, whether paper,

electronic, or otherwise in a secure locked location

under my direct control or with appropriate

safeguards. I hereby further agree that if I have to

use the services of a third party to assist in the

research study, who will potentially have access to

any Confidential Information of participants, that I will

enter into an agreement with said third party prior to

using any of the services, which shall provide at

minimum the confidential obligations set forth herein.

I agree that I will immediately report any known or

suspected breach of this confidential statement

regarding the above research project to the University

of Phoenix, Institutional Review Board.

Michael R. Perez	Michael R. Perez	Jan. 17, 2013
Signature of Researcher	Printed Name	Date
(Redacted for anonymity)	(Redacted for anonymity)	Jan. 17, 2013
Signature of Witness	Printed Name	Date

APPENDIX I
CERTIFICATE OF ORIGINALITY

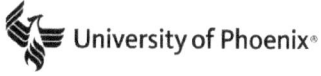 University of Phoenix®

I certify the attached paper is my original work. I am familiar with, and acknowledge my responsibilities, which are part of, the University of Phoenix Student Code of Academic Integrity. I affirm that any section of the paper submitted previously is attributed and cited as such, and this paper has not been submitted by anyone else. I have identified the sources of all information whether quoted verbatim or paraphrased, all images, and all quotations with citations and reference listings. Along with citations and reference listings, I have used quotation marks to identify quotations of fewer than 40 words and have used block indentation for quotations of 40 or more words. Nothing in this assignment violates copyright, trademark, or other intellectual property laws. I further agree my name typed on the line below is intended to have, and shall have, the same validity as my handwritten signature. Student's signature (name typed here is equivalent to a signature):

/s/ Michael R. Perez

INDEX

CURRICULUM VITAE

Michael R. Perez, DM, MPA, BS, AA

Whittier, CA

714-501-9092

michaelrperez5@gmail.com

https://www.linkedin.com/in/michaelperez5

Statement of Teaching Philosophy

My teaching philosophy and reasoning for becoming an adjunct professor is to facilitate online education for working adults, they have vast experience they bring into the classroom, they are diverse and want to learn and apply their varied industry experience. As a traditional and on-line student during my academic career, I find that I can relate to working adults who can be guided to a successful career at any stage of their life. My personal educational journey has led me to a career change from the aerospace industry to education, because of my commitment to students, institution, and learning. Having attended traditional and online institutions I can attest to the rigors of online education. The importance of keeping students engaged in an online environment is motivation to make education appealing and worth the time and effort that adult learners invest.

As professor's it is our duty to facilitate a learning environment for all students, however, it is the student's level of effort that will keep them motivated to learn. My experience with traditional and on-line institutions offers students insight into both delivery methods. It is my responsibility to ensure that I am available to my students when needed and that I am flexible in my schedule and sensitive to each student's needs that could impeded their progress. The online environment can be daunting for those who are not willing to put in the hard work necessary to achieve their educational goals. Ultimately, the responsibility for learning rest with each and every student, and I will do my part to ensure they walk away with an inspired learning experience.

PERSONAL ATTRIBUTES AND QUALIFICATIONS

- Innovative Leader emphasizing personal and professional development.
- Mentoring and coaching with excellent results.
- Excellent Team building skills with practical hands-on experience.
- Creative and innovative approach in the distribution of security services
- Instill confidence in employee problem-solving abilities by having them apply principles learned on the job.
- Flexible and adaptive to change.
- Team player and avid participant with the ability to serve as a catalyst for sustainable change.
- Successful coaching and mentoring employees involved in Integrated Product Teams (IPT) and organizational initiatives.
- Key creator in the development and deployment of a Knowledge Management Initiative for 1,300 Boeing Security & Fire Protection personnel.
- Exceptional project and program management skills.

- Leadership attributes of finding a way, charting the course, setting high expectations, inspiring others, and delivering results.
- Strategic and critical thinking skills.
- Leadership focus on employee training and development to grow skills.
- Successful change leader through disciplined execution to plan.

PROFESSIONAL ADULT TRAINER

Experience training peers, managers, and executives.
Senior Industrial Security Specialist, The Boeing Company

- Developed Knowledge Management program for 117 Security & Fire Protection managers, designed and deployed Knowledge Profiler Tool
  - Knowledge Profiler Tool
  - Knowledge Profiler Instructions

Environment and Platforms

- Coached Process Action Team: Designed for
  Level 1 and 2 industrial security personnel
    - Computer Based Training (CBT) Modules

- Coached Process Action Team: In person training
  module for Level 3 and 4 industrial security
  personnel
    - PowerPoint presentation

- Created Intellectual Currency Protection (ICP)
  program: In person training module 6,000 Boeing
  aerospace personnel.
    - PowerPoint presentation script and
      procedure

PRESENTATIONS TO GROUPS

- Provided security briefings to program personnel
  in preparation of government inspections
    - Defense Security Service (DSS) self-
      inspection briefing

- Provided New Hire Orientation briefing
  - Security Briefing to new personnel

PROFESSIONAL POSITIONS

Senior Industrial Security Specialist
Shared Services Group (SSG)
Boeing Defense Space & Security-Network and
Space Systems (N&SS), El Segundo, CA

- Provide industrial security support to complex new business platforms essential to national security objectives.
- Deliver Security Awareness Training and Education (SATE) to program personnel.
- Assist in review and revision of strategic proposals in support of new business ventures.
- Assist program personnel with daily security operations in support of customer requirements: visits, escorting, foreign travel, foreign contact, and investigations.
- Direct and deliver industrial security services to program personnel in support of new business activities.

Industrial Security Manager

Shared Services Group (SSG)

Boeing Defense Space & Security Huntington Beach, CA

- Managed and delivered security policies, programs, and plans in compliance with government and company initiatives.
- Coordinated Department of Defense (DoD) security inspections and conducted mid cycle self-inspections to ensure National Industrial Security Program Operating Manual (NISPOM) compliance.
- Conducted random audits of classified security procedures and investigated reported security violations and infractions, prepared written documentation of investigative findings.
- Provided leadership and direction to 15 security professionals.
- Built and sustained relationships with business partners and stakeholder

Major Accomplishments:

- Coached and developed 15 industrial security personnel in support of national security objectives.
- Improved processes and increased productivity through cross-training.
- Achieved a Superior DSS VA rating for 2014.
- Received 2014 James S. Cogswell Award for sustained security excellence.
- Implemented Security Awareness, Training, and Education (SATE) best practice.
- Created "Security of the Month" recognition program.
- Management Champion for Affirmative Action program for underrepresented groups.
- Created and implemented Knowledge Management initiative to 1,300 security personnel.
- Created and distributed Knowledge Management Profiler Tool to 117 managers.

Facility Security Officer (FSO)

Shared Services Group (SSG)

Boeing Network & Space Systems El Segundo, CA

- Directed and delivered industrial security services for intelligence and government/commercial space systems.

- Managed and monitored Department of Defense (DoD) programs encompassing the following: information, physical, industrial, communication, operation, personnel, automation security, special category, and foreign disclosure required in the execution of program directives.

- Provided leadership and direction to 8 security professionals in the delivery of security services to 6,000 onsite personnel.

Major Accomplishments:

- Developed and implemented Security Operations Plan to support classified satellite launch operations.

- Coached and developed 8 industrial security personnel in support of satellite launch operations.

- Improved delivery of security services to 6,000

employees, major programs, and security peers.

- Responsible for process improvement and customer service engagement.

- Created Mission Control Center (MCC) Security Manual for improved delivery of services.

- Received Commendable DSS Vulnerability Assessment Rating: 2010 through 2014.

Program Protection Industrial Security Manager

Brigade Combat Team Modernization (BCTM) Program

Boeing Defense, Space & Security (BDS) Huntington Beach, CA

- Directed and delivered industrial security services to Army's Brigade Combat Modernization (BCTM) program to empower soldiers with increased intelligence, reconnaissance, and surveillance capabilities.

- Managed and monitored security disciplines: information, physical, industrial, communication, operation, personnel, automation security, special category, and foreign disclosure required in the execution of program directives.

- Provided Program Security Management guidance across multi-discipline security to include DoD, SCI, and SAP.
- Directed program closure activities at multiple sites across the country in compliance with United States Government contractual requirements.
- Executed compliance assessment reviews and self inspections to ensure compliance with government and company regulations/requirements.

Major Accomplishments:

- Developed and implemented Operations Security (OPSEC) plan for 25 first Tier One Team Partners located across the Continental USA.
- Managed 9 Boeing offsite program facilities supporting BCTM Program activities.
- Integral to Defense Security Service (DSS) Superior award for zero program deficiencies in 2009 and 2010.
- Executed BCTM contract termination to close-out SCI, SAP, and DoD activities at 25 first Tier supplier facilities.

- Implemented LEAN initiatives to redeploy personnel and reduce footprint in underutilized locations.
- Generated and implemented Network Infosec Unit (NIU) Plan to manage and protect Ground Mobile Radio (GMR) at Boeing El Paso and White Sands Missile Range (WSMR).
- Coached Process Action Team (PAT) Instructor Led Training for Level 3 and 4 security personnel.
- Implemented Instructor Led Training sessions for Level 3 and 4 security personnel.
- Coached End of Day Check Process Action Team.
- Executed, implemented, and closed-out over 200 DD254s in accordance with Continuity of Operations (CONOPS) to ensure standardization among One Team Partners (OTP).

Industrial Security Manager and Facility Security Officer (FSO)

Shared Services Group (SSG)

Boeing Defense, Space & Security (BDS), Anaheim, CA

- Managed and administered industrial security policies, programs, and plans for compliance with government and company initiatives for the Boeing Anaheim facility.

- Coordinated Department of Defense (DoD) security inspections and conducted mid cycle self-inspections to ensure National Industrial Security Program Operating Manual (NISPOM) compliance.

- Conducted random audits of classified security procedures and investigated reported security violations and infractions, prepared written documentation of investigative findings.

- Provided leadership direction to 24 Boeing employees and 5 Pinkerton Government Services (PGS) employees in daily security operations.

- Managed industrial security labor budget of 1.5M.

- Evaluated, communicated, and mitigated computing and information security risks.

- Documented and presented approval for Information System Security Plans to Defense Security Services (DSS) representatives.

- Managed and provided oversight of 20+ large scale Department of Defense (DoD) programs critical to national security.

- Conducted investigations in accordance with company and government compliance requirements.
- Executed compliance assessment reviews and self-inspections to ensure compliance with government and company regulations/requirements.

Major Accomplishments:

- Managed compliance of 80 Automated Information System (AIS) Security Plans and Protection Profiles in accordance with Defense Security Service (DSS) NISPOM Chapter 8 requirements.
- Coached and developed 24 industrial security personnel in support of Boeing Defense business objectives.
- Reduced security violations and infractions by 25% through implementation of Security Awareness Training & Education (SATE) Program.
- Developed Logs, Certifications and Requirements (LCARs) system to manage and maintain health of automated information systems within the Boeing

enterprise.

- Implemented LEAN initiatives through cross-training personnel in all security disciplines.
- Coached Process Action Team Computer Based Training (CBT) for Level 1 and 2 security personnel.
- Implemented Computer Based Training (CBT) modules to 500 Security & Fire Protection Government Security Personnel.

GMD Program Security Team Lead

Shared Services Group (SSG)

Boeing Defense, Space & Security (BDS), Anaheim, CA

- Managed and administered industrial security requirements for the Ground-based Midcourse Defense (GMD) Program.
- Coordinated Department of Defense (DoD)/Agency oversight of multiple security disciplines. Interpreted and administered National Industrial Security Program Operating Manual (NISPOM), Export Administration Regulations (EAR), International Traffic in Arms (ITAR) and

multiple security classification guides.

- Managed and mentored 4 industrial security employees in daily program security activities to include: personnel security, DD254s, briefings, investigations, etc.

- Generated and maintained programmatic statistical data, metrics, and processes for senior management review.

- Developed and maintained Security Awareness, Training and Education (SATE) program.

- Interfaced with government customers, suppliers, and company personnel to implement industrial security policy and procedures.

- Executed compliance assessment reviews and self inspections to ensure compliance with government and company regulations/requirements.

Major Accomplishments:

- Created new employee entry/exit process in compliance with program security requirements.
- Implemented Lean initiatives through cross-training and knowledge sharing activities.

- Reduced security reportable security violations by 30% through security awareness, training, and education.

FORMAL EDUCATION

2014, University of Phoenix, Phoenix, AZ

Doctor of Management (DM), Organizational Leadership (OL)

1994, Cal State University Fullerton, Fullerton, CA

Master of Public Administration (MPA), Public Administration-Human Resources

1988, Cal State University Long Beach, Long Beach, CA

Bachelor of Science (BS), Security Administration

1980, Cypress College, Cypress CA

Associate of Arts (AA), General Business

HIGHLY COMPETENT SUBJECT AREAS

Computer Experience

- Information Technology Fluency
- MS Office Suite
- Blackboard
- Unix, Linux
- Windows

Learning Management System Experience

- Analytical
- Business Acumen
- Lead Manage Change
- Team Building
- Strategy Development and Deployment

Subject Matter Expert

- Organizational Leadership
- Public Administration
- Criminal Justice
- Research
- Knowledge Management

Business and Technical Training and Certifications

- Advanced Excel Certificate

PUBLICATIONS, ARTICLES, AND RESEARCH

Perez, M. R. (2015). *Knowledge Transfer by Industrial Security Personnel at a United States-Based Aerospace Company: A Phenomenological Study.* Virginia Beach, VA: D. Boyer Consulting.

Perez, M. R. (2014). *Knowledge transfer by industrial security personnel at a united states-based aerospace company: A phenomenological study* (Order No. 3707408). Available from Dissertations & Theses @ University of Phoenix. (1690464781).

Perez, M. (2011), *Philosophy of Meaning and Value Summary and Application Plan.* Unpublished manuscript. School of Advanced Studies, University of Phoenix, Phoenix, AZ.

Perez, M. (2011*), Organizational Management System.* Unpublished manuscript. School of

Advanced Studies, University of Phoenix, Phoenix,
AZ.

Perez, M. (2011), *Leadership Evaluation.*
Unpublished manuscript. School of Advanced
Studies, University of Phoenix, Phoenix, AZ.

Perez, M. (2011), *Forces or Trends in Leadership,*
Unpublished manuscript. School of Advanced
Studies, University of Phoenix, Phoenix, AZ.

Perez, M. (2011), *Creating an organizational
paradigm,* Unpublished manuscript. School of
Advanced Studies, University of Phoenix, Phoenix,
AZ.

Perez, M. (2010), *Transformational Leadership
Addendum.* Unpublished manuscript. School of
Advanced Studies, University of Phoenix, Phoenix,
AZ.

Perez, M. (2010), *Transformational Leadership
Addendum.* Unpublished manuscript. School of
Advanced Studies, University of Phoenix, Phoenix,
AZ.

Perez, M. (2010), *Shared Leadership: Collaboration.*
Unpublished manuscript. School of Advanced
Studies, University of Phoenix, Phoenix, AZ.

Perez, M. (2010), *Personal Leadership Statement,*

Unpublished manuscript. School of Advanced
Studies, University of Phoenix, Phoenix, AZ.

Perez, M. (2010), *Organizational Leadership and
Team Design*, Unpublished manuscript. School of
Advanced Studies, University of Phoenix, Phoenix,
AZ.

Perez, M. (2010), *Organizational Culture and Team
Effect Paper.* Unpublished manuscript. School of
Advanced Studies, University of Phoenix, Phoenix,
AZ.

Perez, M. (2010), *Organizational Culture and Team
Effect Paper*, Unpublished manuscript. School of
Advanced Studies, University of Phoenix, Phoenix,
AZ.

Perez, M. (2010*), Leadership Evaluation.*
Unpublished manuscript. School of Advanced
Studies, University of Phoenix, Phoenix, AZ.

Perez, M. (2010), *Interview Instrument Development
Experience.* Unpublished manuscript. School of
Advanced Studies, University of Phoenix, Phoenix,
AZ.

Perez, M. (2010), *Evaluating Team Performance*,
Unpublished manuscript. School of Advanced
Studies, University of Phoenix, Phoenix, Arizona.

Perez, M. (2009), *Management Philosophy Comparison*. Unpublished manuscript. School of Advanced Studies, University of Phoenix, Phoenix, AZ.

Perez, M. (2009), *EQ, Management, and Leadership*. Unpublished manuscript. School of Advanced Studies, University of Phoenix, Phoenix, AZ.

PROFESSIONAL AND SCHOLARLY PRESENTATIONS

- Knowledge Management: Knowledge Profiler Tool
- Enterprise Knowledge Management Education and Training of Knowledge Transfer Tools
- Intellectual Currency Protection (ICP) Training
- Defense Security Service (DSS) Vulnerability Assessment In-Brief
- Security Education Awareness Training (SATE) Monthly Briefing
- New Hire Orientation Training (Security)
- Ground-based Midcourse Defense (GMD) New Hire Security Orientation Training

RESIDENCIES AND COLLOQUIA

- DOC/721R-Doctoral Seminar I (3 day residency)
- DOC/731R Collaborative Case Study (5 day residency)
- DOC/732R-Doctoral Seminar III (3 day residency)
- DOC/740R-Annual Renewal Residency (3 day course)

COMMITTEE SERVICE

- National Security Classification Management Society (NCMS)

PROFESSIONAL AFFILIATIONS

- National Classification Management Society (NCMS)
- NCMS Southwest Chapter Committee Chair
- University of Phoenix Mentoring Program Representative

AWARDS AND HONORS

- 2014 James S. Cogswell Award for Security Excellence

COMMUNITY SERVICE

- Boeing Employee Engagement: Community Outreach Volunteer

ABOUT THE AUTHOR

Dr. Michael Perez, author and industrial security professional, has worked in a Security and Fire Prevention organization at a leading United States-based aerospace company in Southern California for 29 years. He was responsible for managing two large scale Department of Defense (DoD) programs during his career.

He has experience in various industrial security disciplines: Program Support, Operations Security (OPSEC), Communication Security (COMSEC), Personnel Security, Physical Security, Computer Security, Special Program Security, Security,

Awareness, Training, and Education (SATE), as a Facility Security Officer (FSO), in Classification Management, International Traffic in Arms (ITAR), and Export Administration Regulations (EA). As an employee with an United States-based aerospace company, he was responsible for implementing a Knowledge Management program for 1,300 employees within the Security and Fire Prevention organization.

His doctorate is in Organizational Leadership (OL), from the University of Phoenix. Dr. Perez is now embarking on a career as an adjunct professor teaching Business Management and Leadership undergraduate and graduate level courses.

Dr. Perez enjoys playing racquetball, working feverishly in the gym, and playing with his two rescue dogs Teddy and Trixie. Michael lives in California with his significant other, Tracy Ann Rico.

Connect with the Author on Social Media and/or

Contact the Author via the following POC:

https://www.facebook.com/michaelperez8

https://www.linkedin.com/in/michaelperez5

ABOUT THE BOOK

This book is designed to provide awareness of the potential loss of knowledge when baby boomers leave their organizations. Over the years the phenomenon of lost knowledge has been discussed repeatedly about the importance of creating robust knowledge management programs. However, corporate strategists are beginning to observe baby boomer departures impacting all industries. This book is important because of the sheer number of retirement eligible employees performing critical functions in myriad industries. Corporations are experiencing significant changes because of the impending baby boomer retirements, with replacements having limited experience and job knowledge.

This book addresses organizational readiness and loss of knowledge when baby boomers retire from their long careers. The problem facing organizations today is their ability to identify, capture, and share critical knowledge before baby boomers retire and take their knowledge with them.

This book will help leaders and managers understand the importance of having a robust knowledge management program. Also, key knowledge transfer areas are discussed: mentoring, communities of practice, and job shadowing to help leaders and managers begin the knowledge transfer journey. This is the only book available about knowledge sharing in a United States-based aerospace company industrial security organization that is transferrable to other industries. As long as companies have baby boomers working for them, they would benefit from reading and implementing knowledge management programs and practices before knowledge walks out the door.

After reading this book, do connect with the author via LinkedIn or Facebook to discuss how the author can be of service to your organization in creating and implementing a knowledge management program. The author is available to discuss employment opportunities in the knowledge management arena.

KEY TERMS IN BOOK: Action learning, Aerospace Industries Association (AIA), Aristotelian Rationalism, baby boom echo, Baby Boomer, best practices, brain drain, Business Continuity, client knowledge, codified knowledge, collective knowledge, Communities of Practice (COP), company culture, cultural values, Delphi method, demographics, Department of Defense (DoD), Domestic Security, Echo Boomers, education, empiricism, employee empowerment, employee knowledge hoarding, Enterprise Fire Protection (EFP), Enterprise Plant Security System (EPSS), Epistemology, ethics, ethnographic study, ethnography, exchange theory, expectancy theory, explicit knowledge, explicit knowledge, follower motivation, Gen-Net, Generation X, Generation Y, global economy, government security director, Hawthorne effect, heritage employees, Hermeneutic Unit (HU), historical research, human capital, human resources, immigration laws, individual knowledge, industrial security, industrial security leaders, Industrial Security Manager (ISM), industrial security specialists, Information Age, Information Technology, informed consent, Infrastructure Security, instrumentation, intellectual capital, intellectual property, intelligence communities, International Security, interpretive phenomenological research, knowledge base, knowledge creation, knowledge development, knowledge drain, knowledge hoarding, knowledge identification, knowledge loss, knowledge management culture, Knowledge Management System, knowledge sharing culture, knowledge transfer, knowledge worker, labor force, layoffs, Leader-Member Exchange Theory, Leaders, leadership development, leadership style, learning model, learning organization, lived experiences, loss of knowledge, loyalty, managers, manual workers, motivation, national security, Nexters, objective existence, observations, operational efficiency, organizational boundaries, organizational leaders, organizational theorists, organizational transformation, patents, personal knowledge, personnel, phenomenological methodology, phenomenological research, pilot study, Plato, Process Action Teams (PAT), process improvements, procurement, program closures, psychology, qualitative research, rationalism, reciprocity, redeployments, Reduction in Force (RIF), reliability, restructuring, retirement, scientific thought, Secret Compartmented Information (SCI), Security and Fire Protection (S&FP), security clearance, security knowledge, security services, Shared Services Group (SSG), silo mentality, skills gap, social costs, social exchange theory, sociology, sourcing strategies, Special Access Program (SAP), Special Access Program (SAP), special program security, strategic benefit, structural descriptions, Subject Matter Expert (SME), subject matter experts (SME), supplier management, tacit knowledge, team lead, technical complexity, technical knowledge, terminations, textural descriptions, theory of knowledge, Top Secret Clearance, Traditionalist, training, Transactional Leadership, Transformational Leadership, trust, typology of knowledge, Uniformed Security, van Kaam technique, virtual workspace, workforce

**Publishing Services
Virginia Beach, VA 23464**

http://dboyerconsulting.com
Dawn@DBoyerConsulting.com

www.ingramcontent.com/pod-product-compliance
Lightning Source LLC
Chambersburg PA
CBHW051849170526
45168CB00001B/41